PENGUIN BOOKS

FOLLOWING FISH

By dint of both circumstance and choice, Samanth Subramanian is a journalist. He has an undergraduate degree in journalism from Pennsylvania State University and a Master's in international relations from Columbia University. By preference, he gravitates towards the long-form, narrative version of journalism—waning today, but still rewarding and revealing to both writers and readers. He has written, among other publications, for *Mint*, the *Far Eastern Economic Review*, *Foreign Policy*, *The New Republic*, *Foreign Affairs*, *The National* and *The Hindu*. This is his first book.

Following Fish

Travels around The Indian Coast

Samanth Subramanian

PENGUIN BOOKS

PENGUIN BOOKS

Published by the Penguin Group

Penguin Books India Pvt. Ltd, 11 Community Centre, Panchsheel Park, New Delhi 110 017, India

Penguin Group (USA) Inc., 375 Hudson Street, New York, New York 10014, USA

Penguin Group (Canada), 90 Eglinton Avenue East, Suite 700, Toronto, Ontario, M4P 2Y3, Canada (a division of Pearson Penguin Canada Inc.)

Penguin Books Ltd, 80 Strand, London WC2R 0RL, England

Penguin Ireland, 25 St Stephen's Green, Dublin 2, Ireland (a division of Penguin Books Ltd)

Penguin Group (Australia), 250 Camberwell Road, Camberwell, Victoria 3124, Australia (a division of Pearson Australia Group Pty Ltd)

Penguin Group (NZ), 67 Apollo Drive, Rosedale, Auckland 0632, New Zealand (a division of Pearson New Zealand Ltd)

Penguin Group (South Africa) (Pty) Ltd, 24 Sturdee Avenue, Rosebank, Johannesburg 2196, South Africa

Penguin Books Ltd, Registered Offices: 80 Strand, London WC2R 0RL, England

First published by Penguin Books India 2010

Copyright © Samanth Subramanian 2010

12 11 10 9 8 7 6 5

ISBN: 9780143064473

Typeset in Sabon MT by Eleven Arts, New Delhi
Printed at Replika Press Pvt. Ltd, Sonepat

To my parents,
who taught me to write and to read,
for which I can never thank them enough.

Rise, brothers, rise! The wakening skies
pray to the morning light.
The wind lies asleep in the arms of the dawn
like a child that has cried all night.
Come, let us gather our nets from the shore
and set our catamarans free,
To capture the leaping wealth of the tide,
for we are the kings of the sea!
No longer delay, let us hasten away
in the track of the sea gull's call,
The sea is our mother, the cloud is our brother,
the waves are our comrades all.
What though we toss at the fall of the sun
where the hand of the sea-god drives?
He who holds the storm by the hair,
will hide in his breast our lives.
Sweet is the shade of the cocoanut glade,
and the scent of the mango grove,
And sweet are the sands at the full o' the moon
with the sound of the voices we love;
But sweeter, O brothers, the kiss of the spray
and the dance of the wild foam's glee;
Row, brothers, row to the edge of the verge,
where the low sky mates with the sea.

The Coromandel Fishers, Sarojini Naidu

CONTENTS

INTRODUCTION

When I was twelve years old, and we were living in Indonesia, my sister and I once accompanied my parents to one of the regular dinner parties that anchored the calendar of the Indian expatriate. As per routine, we were shunted off upstairs with our friends, to watch television and play video games. Our parents sat downstairs with the other parents, probably to complain about how all their children did these days was watch television and play video games.

Summoned for dinner an hour or so later, we came down into the dining room, to a large table laden with various plates of food. My memory seems to have captured this scene and then, like a rogue design editor, Photoshopped it into even sharper significance. The peripheral details of the other dishes are blurred, but the centrepiece of the table remains in vivid focus. It was a whole, steamed fish, coloured such a wretched gray that it reminded me instantly of death. I also recall a smell that lurked over the table like an invisible warning. I did not eat much dinner that night.

Taste is the most temperamental of our senses, remarkably resilient in some ways but also malleable enough for one to be repulsed for life by a single experience. That dinner party was sufficient to put me off fish for the next decade, and even in my early twenties, when I cautiously began venturing back towards seafood, I stuck wherever possible to the safe, taste-slaying possibilities of batter and the deep fryer. Fish and chips I could face, but not fish in soup, or fish baked or grilled or, worst of all, steamed. This was not as restricting as it sounds. Everybody else in my family is rigidly vegetarian, and I was happy enough with poultry and meat when I ate out.

Depending on how you look at it, this makes me either the least ideal or the most ideal person to write about fish. Naturally, I prefer to take the latter view, and to believe that being unencumbered by dense schools of fish-related memories is a distinct advantage. But this book goes beyond considering fish merely as food. Particularly in a nation with as lengthy and diverse a coastline as India's, fish can sit at the heart of many worlds—of culture, of history, of sport, of commerce, of society. It can knit the coast together in one dramatic swoop: The hilsa, pride and joy of Bengal, now often arrives in many fish markets from Gujarat, at the very opposite end of the coastline. Or it can fragment the coast into a multitude of passions and traditions, each different from the one found a hundred kilometres to the north or south of it. Looking more closely at even one aspect of these worlds is like picking up the most visible thread of a fishing net, and suddenly seeing the entire skein lift into view.

Much as I would have liked to begin in Kolkata and ramble right around the edges of the Indian peninsula over several continuous months, I wasn't able to travel that way. Instead, I tore large chunks of time out of my working life, which is possibly why the journey divided itself easily into individual segments, and thence into individual chapters. I flew a lot. I also took buses and motorcycles and trains and cars, dozens of auto-rickshaws (including one that I drove, rather poorly, on a deserted Kerala highway), many flimsy-looking boats, twice a bicycle, and once a jerry-rigged motor vehicle for which no technical term exists.

Almost always, I travelled alone, and so I came to depend on the kindnesses of people who knew people who knew my friends. They would ease my entry into alien worlds, at least initially; when I didn't follow the language, they would translate and add helpful annotations. In their comforting shadow, emboldened by the fact that they belonged even if I didn't, I could loiter endlessly, watching and listening, starting up dialogues where I chose. In this way, I aspired to become what V. S. Naipaul once called 'a discoverer of people, a finder-out of stories.'

In pottering about the Indian coast and writing about it, I have not intended to produce a guide to lead others down the same route. This is, in that sense, not a how-to-travel book but a travelogue—a record of my journeys, my experiences and observations, my conversations with the people I met, and my investigations into subjects that I happened to find incredibly fascinating. Put another way, it is simply what I believe all travel writing to be in its absolute essence: plain, old-fashioned journalism, disabuser of notions, destroyer of preconceptions, discoverer of the relative, shifting nature of truth.

New Delhi
January 2010

1

On hunting the hilsa and mastering its bones

A day before I arrived in Kolkata, Burrabazar began to burn. Fire ate through fourteen levels of the Nandaram Market complex and its adjoining shops, and late in the evening, I fancied that the smoke still slept in the air. It wasn't just because of traffic smog that I struggled to read a green-on-white sign mounted on a building, or to spot the little toenail clipping of a moon; I genuinely sensed the acridity of fresh smoke. Later, a friend's father informed me that what I smelled was the burning of leaves, a popular winter-evening pastime much like dog walking or badminton. (That green-on-white sign, by the way, turned out to announce the premises of the Pollution Control Board.)

Smouldering vegetation notwithstanding, I'd been reliably told that winter is the best time to visit Kolkata. The weather behaves itself and moves into a Goldilocks state—not hot but not too cold, not humid but not too dry. The pace of life slackens even by Kolkata standards, tempers are more even, the traffic seems tolerable, and the puchkas taste better. What winter is not a good time for, they told me, is to eat hilsa, and as this is all that I wanted to do, Kolkata and I appeared to be at odds with each other. At every turn, Bengali classicists—and there are many of them—suggested gently that I return for hilsa in the monsoon. There are no hilsa to be had now, they would state definitively— at least, no hilsa worth the eating. Grit your teeth, make it through the next few months, and come back then. The hilsa, they implied, is simultaneously a fish and a lesson in moral science: Good things come to those who wait.

But Kolkata's fish barons, far less classicist, have decided that fish are more lucrative than morals. In mid-January, I found hilsa everywhere I looked. Restaurants produced it without a murmur of protest, droves of trucks bore it in from Bangladesh, riverside shack eateries pressed it upon me, and fish markets teemed with it. Good things came to those who had even Rs 60 in their wallets. Which was how, less than three hours after I first coughed on leaf smoke, I was sitting with a plate of rice and a shallow dish of shorshe ilish in front of me.

If Bengali cuisine were Wimbledon, the hilsa would always play on Centre Court. It is the undisputed champion of fish in this corner of India, possessed of enigmatic qualities of taste and all the more desired because of its vaunted seasonal elusiveness. Poets have written on it, one calling the ilish, as the hilsa is known in Bengali, 'the darling of the waters.' The hilsa can be a symbol of Bengali identity but also of the sibling rivalry between East and West Bengal. It participates in another rivalry as well: A hilsa dinner is a tradition for fans of the East Bengal football team when it wins, just as prawns are for fans of Mohun Bagan. At every fish bazaar, in a pleasing spot of meta-fishing, the promise of fresh hilsa is bait for customers, shouted out to reel business in.

For many years, my immediate mental reference point to the phrase 'fish market' has been the admonition of the teachers at my school in Chennai, many of whom had clearly never been to such a market. During particularly raucous afternoons, the teacher would sally forth, in rhetorical spirit: 'Where do you think you are? A fish market?' I remember I would pause at the time, suspending my hijinks sometimes for a whole second, to quickly imagine a deafening charnel house where one waded through rivers of blood and offal, battled piercing odours, and purchased fish from beetle-browed, thuggish merchants of death.

The Lake Market fish stalls rose far above those infernal expectations. In one long space papered over with wall prints of Shiva and Kali, appropriate deities of destruction, the vendors sat behind their fish on concrete platforms. Cutters jutted out from under their knees, their dark blades rising like the trunks of trumpeting elephants. Melting ice and blood dripped in taut rivulets into the gutters that lined the aisles. At the corner of each platform, fish innards stacked up in neat pyramids. The fish was so fresh there was barely any odour; the solitary line of chicken vendors at the far wall was entirely responsible for the atmosphere's redolence. Most notably, though, business was conducted at a very civilized volume; my teachers, I think, would have been suitably astonished.

Khokon, my gaunt and bescarved guide, was the first to assure me that there was now good hilsa to be had even in the off-season in Kolkata, and he marched me towards a vendor to prove it. The traditional start of the hilsa season, Saraswathi Pooja, was still over a month away. That is when the fish, sea-dwellers for the rest of the year, begin to move house in large numbers, swimming upriver to spawn. But there are hilsa to be found in the rivers in winter as well; one theory has it, in fact, that eco-savvy Bengalis of earlier centuries constructed the idea of the hilsa 'season' and buckled it to the religious calendar only to avoid overfishing.

In my hands, the proffered hilsa felt firm, dense and oily. Its fine silver scales were not immediately obvious to the touch, but they still glinted, under the low overhead lamps, like a tray of precious gems. All the hilsa in the market that day, each between eight hundred grams and one and a half kilogrammes, were from Bangladesh, and they wouldn't have been there even ten days earlier. The Bangladesh government, in response to high domestic demand, had imposed a six-month ban on exports to India, and the ban had run its course a week before I reached Kolkata, when fish shipments resumed across the Benapole–Petrapole border.

As united as they are in appreciation of the hilsa, Bengalis are divided by geography over the relative merits of hilsa from the Padma and Ganga rivers. Bangladeshis prize the plumper fish from the Padma above everything else; the Ganga hilsa, they will concede magnanimously, is still hilsa, but that is really all that can be said for it. West Bengalis, on the other hand, look with sympathy upon their oriental cousins, who cannot appreciate the intense flavours of the Ganga hilsa; their collective opinion is that the Bangladeshis are more to be pitied than scorned for their congenital error in judgement.

At the Lake Market bazaar, the fish vendors claimed that they could tell Ganga hilsa from Padma hilsa simply by touch. How? 'The Indian fish looks more silvery,' one sage began, but then suddenly, like a stricken Freemason on the verge of divulging the secret handshake, he gave up, and hinted instead at a mystic art. 'It's in the touch, you won't understand it,' he said elliptically. 'Just as you can't tell if somebody is a good person or a bad person by just looking at their face. You need to know fish; you need to have that experience.'

His younger, non-Templar neighbour had fewer qualms. 'The Padma fish are oilier, and I have a theory for that. There is more silt in the Ganga, so the fish are leaner, since they fight against the silt and the current to swim upstream.' The Padma fish, happily deprived of this workout, thus turned out plumper and rounder. 'And then there is also a pronounced pink streak on the underbelly of the Bangladeshi fish,' he added, helpfully pointing it out to me by tracing a smear of pinkness with a chipped fingernail.

I began to move on, but my vendor seemed at a loose end, eager to chat. 'How come it isn't busier than it is right now?' I asked. It was already 10 a.m., but there were still baskets of shrimp and crab, pre-filleted hilsa, and monster-sized catla spread out on banana leaves, awaiting buyers. 'It's a Monday,' he said. 'Very few people buy fish on a Monday.'

This puzzled me. It wasn't a religious stricture, as far as I could tell, and nobody seemed to know any other reason for fishless Mondays. Weeks later, though, I lit upon one possible solution. In *Kitchen Confidential*, the New York chef Anthony Bourdain advises his readers never to order fish in a restaurant on Monday. At the beginning of the week, a restaurant chef is still trying to move out the fish left over from the weekend. 'He anticipates the likelihood that he might still have some fish lying around on Monday morning—and he'd like to get money for it without poisoning his customers,' Bourdain explains. 'If it still smells okay on Monday night—you're eating it.' Forewarned, especially in the case of dodgy fish, is forearmed.

Shorshe ilish, perhaps the most popular technique of cooking hilsa, involves simmering and serving cuts of the fish in a mustard sauce so pungent that its wallop reaches right into your sinuses. The sauce is a marvellous assembly of grainy mustard, curd, chillies, turmeric and lemon, achieving the sort of bright yellow that is otherwise only found in pots of poster paint. But its very power always leaves room for regret that it might be masking the natural creamy taste of the fish.

The first time I ate shorshe ilish, however, I thought no such thing; I was too focussed on making sure that the bones didn't kill me. The hilsa has a viciously designed skeleton, evolution's way of convincing predators that they should look elsewhere for lunch. Like an overbuilt house, its superstructure has big support bones, feathery little bones called thorns that tickle as they slide accidentally down your throat, and a host of other innocuous bones that seem to serve no purpose but that can probably puncture your digestive system once swallowed. 'The Bengalis have a standing joke,' Sharad Dewan, the executive chef at the Park hotel in Kolkata, told me. 'A true Bengali can take a mouthful of hilsa, and sort meat from bone in his mouth, swallowing the meat and storing the bones to one side, to be extricated later. If you can't do that, you're not a real Bengali.'

Dewan is a New Delhi man himself, and he first ate hilsa at the house of a friend in that city's Bengali enclave of Chittaranjan Park. 'I remember how they would cook the entire fish. Not one part was wasted,' said Dewan. 'The evening would start with fried hilsa, and then there would be a curry with mustard, and then little cutlets of hilsa roe. If I ever spent the night there, I'd wake up the next morning to see breakfast that used up the fish's head—either in a soupy stock called jhol or mashed up into a chutney.' The chutney, called ambol ilish, involves deep-frying the head, breaking it up into little pieces, and marinating them in raw tamarind, sugar, lemon juice and the Bengali five-spice mixture known as panch phoran.

If you can wangle your way into it—I couldn't—the best place in Kolkata to eat hilsa, by popular opinion, is the exclusive Bengal Club. But Dewan's kitchen at the Park is not far behind. My hilsa education got suddenly intensive under one of his lieutenants, Vasanthi, whose relaxed, toothy grin completely belied her swift hands, her alert eyes, and her martinet manner with a gangling assistant.

'First, we learn to cut.' Cutting into a hilsa feels very much like cutting into a very firm, fresh tomato. First a swipe near the neck, then near the tail, and then longitudinal cuts along the sides to peel away the fillet from that side of the fish. This particular hilsa had gorgeous, pink, slightly marbled flesh. 'Each fillet has a little black area at the bottom, lining the belly of the fish,' said Vasanthi. 'Cut that off. It tastes of nothing.' With another fish, we lopped off the head and, through the digestive orifice, scooped out a mass of congealed blood and hilsa innards. Then we cut the fish into thick slices—what Vasanthi called 'curry cuts'—to fry. 'In Bengal, we keep the fins on, we don't cut them off,' said Vasanthi. 'And look here, this is the roe. You can prise it out and fry it up with mustard, onions and green chillies.' Around the liver sat ruddy flaps of fat, signs of a hilsa that had led a contented life. 'That liver would be great to fry.'

Somebody, somewhere, must have thrown a switch at this point, because Vasanthi's actions moved up two gears, and as she whipped between ingredients, my notes began to get scratchier and scratchier. For a baked dish of mint hilsa, she salted one fillet, mixed some mint chutney with what must have been curd (although my scribbles say 'crud'), mustard oil and desiccated coconut, and marinated the fish in the mixture for ten minutes. She popped the covered plate into a microwave set for eight minutes, power-napped for three seconds, and then turned to the shorshe ilish.

Even on warp speed, Vasanthi made the best shorshe ilish I ate in all my days in Kolkata, days that were so full of shorshe ilish that they now seem to meld together in memory into one bright yellow, mustardy, sinus-rattling streak. 'To make the mustard paste ahead of time, you soak black and yellow mustard in water, with chillies, for half an hour, and you grind that into a paste. Not too fine, just grainy,' she said. To that paste, she added curd, turmeric, salt and lemon. 'Add that immediately after grinding,' she warned sternly, somehow sensing that I was exactly the sort of person to dally with a curd-lemon-turmeric mixture in my hand. 'Delay it even by a few seconds, and the paste turns bitter.'

In a wok, she heated mustard oil and then added, in succession, the mustard paste, water, slices of halved green chillies, salt, quartered tomatoes, and finally, two curry cuts of the hilsa. While the shorshe ilish slowly simmered its way to completion, Vasanthi rolled two other cuts of the fish in the mustard paste and allowed them to marinate. When they were ready, she wrapped them in banana leaves and let them steam in a colander for twenty minutes, like two fat gentlemen, draped in Turkish towels, sweating in a sauna. 'This is ilish paturi, a very popular, very classical dish,' she said. The fish were barely in the colander, and she was already tracing patterns on the cutting-board with her knife, itching to move on.

Where Vasanthi really came into her own was in deboning hilsa fillets, a practice that has become popular only in the recent past, to tempt inept non-Bengalis who cannot sieve bones in their mouths. Laying the steamed, softened, mint-crusted fillet flat, she cut it into four long quarters. Then, pressing down hard with her knife, she moved an entire quarter of meat off its skeleton. This is a tricky maneuver; you can take away too little flesh and leave much of the hilsa still sitting on its bones, or you can scrape too hard and take dozens of little thorn-bones out with the flesh. Vasanthi wielded her knife with the delicacy of an archaeologist dusting skeletal remains, careful to leave behind nothing but bone.

The final act was also the most straightforward. Firing up another burner with a loud 'whooooomph,' Vasanthi set on it a non-stick pan laced liberally with mustard oil. Into that went two cuts of hilsa, dusted with just salt and turmeric, to be fried until a golden-brown sheath crept across the surface of the fish. The fish she spooned out, and the oil she set aside. The hilsa is a naturally fatty fish, and in a wok, the heat forces its oils out, to mix with the mustard oil. The hilsa-enhanced mustard oil is worth saving, to flavour food or even to mix simply with rice, as many Bengalis do.

Vasanthi's plump hilsa, on the day, were from Bangladesh, and what they seemed to lack in sharp natural flavour, they made up for in texture. The paturi, unwrapped like a Christmas gift, flaked away in soft layers, its creamy flesh touched with the mustard and tempered by the damp, green taste of the banana leaf. The fried cuts of hilsa, under their crisp swagger, were softies at heart, fresh and warm. I may have done the shorshe ilish some injustice, though. Entranced by its grainy, wicked gravy, I neglected to take any more than passing bites of the fish, although its oils—essence de hilsa—had swept like a marauding army through the gravy anyway.

My vigilance lulled by a gourmandizing stupor, I could thus turn to the deboned mint hilsa, knowing that even the most careless of bites wouldn't result in bleeding gums or a lacerated tongue. But after many days of eating hilsa for breakfast, lunch and dinner, my bone-seeking sense seemed to remain automatically alert, and that turned out to be a blessing. In one—and only one—mouthful of hilsa, I bit down gently and landed upon a mass of thorns in the middle of the flesh, emerging from the fish in deadly little tendrils.

I suspended chewing and pondered the situation. Then I began to work at the mouthful of fish with my tongue, holding the bones steady against my teeth or the roof of my mouth and coaxing hilsa off them in patient little moves. To an observer, I must have resembled a cow meditatively considering its cud. I was left, at the end of my exertions, with just a jumbled clutch of bones, which I neatly deposited to one side of my plate. I ate the rest of my mint hilsa in a glow of satisfaction. It was one of the proudest moments of my life.

The Park hotel gets much of its hilsa, and other fish, from the Howrah wholesale market, and I had been hoodwinked into believing that the action there began at 3 a.m. When I arrived at five past three on a cold morning, though, there was exactly one truck in situ, its plastic crates and wicker baskets of ice-fraught fish being unloaded onto long handcarts or onto makeshift cushions of folded cloth atop the heads of willing porters. The next truck would not arrive until 4 a.m., and at that morning's temperature, an hour was a long time to stand around in open-toed sandals.

The Howrah fish market is a labyrinth of open-fronted shops that looks forbidding when unlit. A bridge running overhead serves as a roof for some of the stalls, with divisions bricked in to separate them. The unloading happens just outside the labyrinth, by the glow of scattered sodium streetlamps, in the underpass beneath the bridge. Between 3 a.m. and 4 a.m., though, not much transpires. I eavesdropped on one loud argument, where a gentleman contended either that fish had been brought here by mistake instead of being taken to the Sealdah market, or had been taken to Sealdah by mistake instead of being brought here—I couldn't figure out which. In my spare time, I gazed at cracked posters of a film called *AIDS and Blind Sex*, a movie that actually looked like it was promoting the virtues of both pursuits.

Around 4 a.m., the bridge's belly began to echo every five or six minutes with the rumble of an incoming truck, and the unloading quickened into the sort of industry that is tiring even to watch. Cartons marked 'Fis' would descend from the trucks, ride into the bowels of the labyrinth, emerge vacant minutes later, and would hustle back onto the beds of the trucks with a satisfying clatter. Everybody worked, so I, walking around aimlessly with a notebook, was a noticeable aberration in the scheme of things. Porters started to stop and ask, curiously:

'*Maal aapka hai?*' Were the goods mine? At first I demurred, not wanting to be mistaken for a fish baron. But this seemed to confound the porters even more, so I opted for a curt half-nod that left the matter open to interpretation.

At half past four, the market began to come to life in a concentric fashion, first awakening in the centre and then radiating outwards in waves of activity. Fish began to go both ways, now leaving in small retail batches as well. Owners opening up their stalls for the morning would rise and stretch, scratch, and then look over their standing orders of fish that had been deposited while they were still asleep. A grumble was almost obligatory: 'He's delivered more ice than fish in this crate, the rascal,' or 'I can't even see these fish, they're so small.' They would holler for the boy selling tea, wrap a ceremonial agarbatti around the rim of their balance pans to consecrate the day's sale, and only then scout the growing crowd for prospective buyers.

Howrah was clearly a seller's market. The vendors laid out baskets of white-bellied pomfret, catla at least the size of adolescent sharks, Bangladeshi hilsa on ice, and little sharks. When crates of shrimp arrived, they were tipped onto the muddy floor of the market and shovelled into weighing pans for sale. There was next to no negotiation. A buyer sidled up, wrapped in a muffler and clutching a standard-issue striped cloth or plastic bag. The vendor barked out his day's prices as a statement and then lay in wait, like a spider in its web, watching his prey engage in an internal debate. He could take it, or he could leave it; when he left it, the vendor indifferently watched him walk away, and then turned to bark at the next internal debater.

Wandering from stall to stall, I could put my hilsa education to test. Every single specimen was soft and plump, with the telltale streak of pink across its underbelly; they were all from Bangladesh, having ridden trucks through the night to arrive at

Hilsa—*always a fish stall's star turn*

Howrah from Petrapole. They were also the pride of every stall's exhibit, placed front and centre on deep beds of ice. 'They're fantastic hilsa,' one vendor told me, although I doubt he would have told me differently even if they'd been laced with arsenic. He then asked me if I owned a fish shop. I reprised my trusty half-nod and moved on.

Dawn broke at twenty minutes to six, and some moments later, the first woman walked into the market. By then, every stall had opened, and the market was an orchestra of sound: the sotto scrape of crates being dragged, the fortissimo yodel of fish prices, the cymbal-crashes of balance pans, the persistent notes of conversation that stayed in the background like second or third violins, and the occasional tuba-like burst of the horn of a truck waiting to be unloaded. By half past six, though, that overture had given way to the rest of the concert, as Kolkata awoke and the noise of traffic washed over the market, as it would until nightfall and beyond.

Despite the pessimism of the Bengali classicists, I managed to eat inordinate amounts of hilsa in Kolkata. At the upscale Oh! Calcutta, I ordered my first boneless hilsa, smothered with a smoky-sweet sauce that failed spectacularly in masking the aggressive, dense taste of hilsa fat. On Mirza Ghalib Road, in New Market, I encountered my first hilsa egg in a dish of shorshe ilish. It looked, at first glance, vaguely like a kidney. The 'egg' was really a fused mass of thousands of little eggs, compact and veined with slender black lines. It tasted chewy on the tongue, crumbling into granules with every bite. Eaten thus from the hilsa, I decided that it was an acquired taste, although I could well see how Vasanthi's fry-up with onions and green chillies would work.

The proprietor of that establishment, Bhupen Shah, was a small, round, soft man, rather like a Padma hilsa himself. He had settled in Kolkata decades ago, but he had grown up in Bangladesh, near a point on the Padma that is reputed to yield particularly good hilsa. 'When I was young, the Padma was deeper, and there were more fish to be had,' he said. Then, as if to ensure some sort of evenhandedness, he added: 'The Ganga doesn't have as many fish now either. The silting and the pollution, you see. The fish come into the river, and they begin to die. And the fish you do catch, they're smaller now. They're not as good to eat either.'

The deterioration of the hilsa was a lament I heard often. No food, of course, is ever as good as it was in one's childhood, but the increasingly muddied and polluted Ganga, and the unchecked overfishing that was providing me with hilsa even in January, have had their effect. 'Earlier, the fish would swim as far as seventy kilometres upriver,' one Howrah fish-seller told me. 'Now they barely make it twenty kilometres inland from the sea.' Even looking at the River Hooghly is instructional. At Kolkata, of course, it looks like a densely polluted, choked river, but even from Kolaghat, across and up the river in the district of East Medinipur, the Hooghly resembles a static ribbon of silt solution. The fishermen of Kolaghat trawl a tributary, the

Rupnarayan, which looks just as muddy, just as hostile to aquatic life.

In season, Kolaghat is famous for its hilsa. Into its pinched streets, the fish-sellers said, cars from Kolkata arrive daily, sent by government officials or corporate executives just to pick up the best of the day's catch. The daily market is the town's centrepiece. For streets together, cereal-sellers sit surrounded by sacks of six or eight types of cereals; fisherwomen with toes reddened by fish blood squat behind cutters, little steel tubs of still-swimming catfish, and turmeric-smeared cuts of fish; on blue tarpaulin, vegetable-sellers arrange potatoes, gourds, red onions, beans both broad and French, big and little eggplants, pumpkins, and huge heads of cabbage. The market consumes half of Kolaghat's day; after it closes, even though it is only mid-afternoon, a cloud of lethargy descends over the town, until the market reopens the next morning.

(It struck me, listening to sales patter in the middle of the Kolaghat market, that India must be the only country in the world where even the word for its currency changes from region to region. In Kolaghat, the fisherwomen used 'takas' for 'rupees,' even if that is really the currency of another country altogether. The word 'rupee' twists and bends into 'rupye,' which sounds like the Indonesian 'rupiah,' into 'rooba,' into 'rupailu,' into 'rupai.' The proportion of Indians using the official 'rupee' in daily life must be very small indeed.)

The hilsa on sale at Kolaghat looked perfunctory rather than appetizing, as if they were present only because a Bengali fish stall wouldn't be a Bengali fish stall without hilsa. There were no Bangladeshi imports here. The bigger hilsa, caught a couple of days ago at sea and stored on ice, felt too soft, their flesh not yet firmed up under the scales. The little ones, referred to in colloquial Bengali as 'small boys,' had been hauled out of the river, but they were wan and thin, plucked too early in their lifecycle to be any good. And yet it was almost always the first of the fish to disappear, a mad hilsa-lust seeming to counter every ounce of received wisdom about fish-buying. The pulse of the Kolaghat market was all about hilsa; in conclusion, as if cosmically arranged, we watched two young men pass by us on a bicycle, and the pillion-rider mused loudly to his companion: 'Without eating hilsa, my mood for the day isn't right at all.'

The other spot close to Kolkata that is famous for its hilsa is Diamond Harbour, where sea trawlers often unload their catch directly to retailers and thence, very quickly, to eateries. Diamond Harbour is fifty-five kilometres from the city, but on the day after Sankranti, thousands of people were still hurtling towards the mela at Gangasagar, where the river meets the sea. The two-hour drive, I was told, would take four hours or possibly more. So instead, I took the standing-room-only train from Ballygunge Junction, filled with whooping students, a highly sought-after peanut vendor called Shumit-da, and another gentleman who sold a mysterious drink in a Sprite bottle that opened with a report like a revolver's.

Diamond Harbour consists essentially of one curving main road, hugging the riverfront, with a Mashal Mustard Oil sponsored embankment that has poison ivy growing out of its cracks. A fleet of jerry-rigged cycle rickshaws, with the traditional two-seater carriage ripped out and replaced by a slatted wooden platform, ferries people for Rs 10 a piece to the Diamond Harbour esplanade. (Swinging your legs en route is a bad idea. You may accidentally clip an elderly Diamond Harbour pedestrian on his shins, and receive a stream of invective that makes your rickshaw-driver laugh. It has been known to happen.)

The esplanade seemed to be popular, on the day, as a picnic spot. Buses and vans coasted to a stop regularly on the shoulder of the road, and families tumbled out for lunch or a snack, or even to just sit on the esplanade benches and take in the spectacular view of the river mouth, broad and blue and twinkling fiercely in the sun. Across from the esplanade, on the other side of the road, was a row of shacks, unnamed eateries that I'd been told would do the hilsa true justice. I'd also been told, by the same person, that innards of asbestos would help, which seemed to entirely contradict the earlier observation.

I wandered into one shack and sat down. 'Shorshe ilish?' 'Shorshe ilish.' From a shelf behind a curtain, a man took out a steel plate filled with rice, two oblong pieces of boiled potato, and a saucer of some thin yellow water that may or may not have started life as daal. The flies came gratis. This was prep kitchen taken to its most extreme; I half-expected a saucer of shorshe ilish to be extracted from under the table or out of a shirt pocket.

Instead, my line chef's wife creaked into action. She walked to a little refrigerator and pulled open its door—quite literally, for the entire door came off its hinges, to be set neatly to one side. From a compartment that, in a conventional fridge, would have been its freezer, she took out a bag of fish cuts, and casually leaned the door back against the fridge.

'Is the fish fresh?'

'Oh, of course, of course. It was brought in just this morning. Ganga hilsa. It'll be very good. You wait and watch.'

She fired up one of the two burners on her stove, washed and set a pan on the flame, and tipped some mustard oil into it. She dusted two cuts of the fish with turmeric, dropped them into the oil, and threw in some red chilli powder for good measure. Meanwhile, her line chef must have begun to fret that it had been too long since the curtain entered into the production. Like Hamlet probing behind his arras, he lifted it aside and, with a look of deep satisfaction, produced a large bowl of oil-slicked, pre-prepared mustard gravy.

The meal should have had nothing going for it. (The rice and potato and yellow water certainly didn't. After my first tentative bite, I didn't touch them.) And yet, by the weird process of alchemy that makes roadside food as great as it is, the shorshe ilish was remarkable. The hilsa, as it fried, smelled divine, and my chef then dropped the pieces into their mustard bath, simmered them rapidly, and spooned them out into a stainless steel saucer. I could still see the black shells of whole mustard spluttered into the gravy. It was hot and peppery, and without the rice, the shorshe ilish became a perfect fish soup.

The hilsa, when it had cooled down enough to be eaten, was firm and chewy, less oily and more intense than anything else I'd eaten. No silvery rings of fat encircled the flesh, and the cuts were smaller and less meaty. Surely this wasn't Bangladeshi hilsa?

'No, it's from the river. It was caught just this morning.'

'But is there hilsa in the river now, this early in the year?'

'Sometimes,' she shrugged. 'You got lucky.'

Later, I crossed the road to sit on one of the stone benches. It was around four in the afternoon, and across the river, where the sun would soon set, I could see the faint outlines of East Medinipur. On the river, trawlers and dinghies placidly ploughed through the waters. A few kilometres south, India's most revered river washed out to sea, expending itself after its mighty march across the plains. To my fancy, the long, magnificent necklace of India's coastline began, in a sense, here—perhaps, even from my little bench on the esplanade.

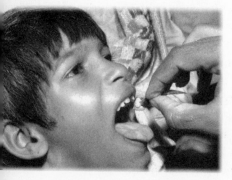

2
On swallowing
a live fish

For many years, even well into his sightless eighties, my paternal grandfather used to practise an art that must be called 'faith healing,' but only because it was predicated on his faith and because it healed. Nobody in my family knows exactly where or how he absorbed this art, and only my father can even attempt to explain how it works. But the Tamil verb for his actions, *mandrikardhu*, sounded so much like the name of the *Indrajal Comics* hero Mandrake the Magician that, at some point in my childhood, I conflated my grandfather's art with Mandrake's magic.

Whenever my grandfather came to stay with us, I'd have the opportunity to linger and watch him at work. He would sit opposite the patient, both on low wooden planks, he bare-chested and buzzing with health, the patient querulous but always eager to believe. My grandfather would shut his eyes and collapse into a little trance, his lips whispering noiselessly. Then he would, with his index finger, trace a host of mysterious prayers into a brass platter of *vibhuthi*, sacred ash, placed in front of him. The patient, meanwhile, would sit on in silence.

A few further minutes into the process, my grandfather's moving finger, having writ, would move on no more. He would palm a few pinches of the ash and, filling his cheeks, blow it all over the patient. Then he would draw a thumbprint of ash in a streak across the patient's forehead, demand an open mouth, and drop in a peck of ash. What remained on the salver would be folded into neat sachets made of old newspapers, to be consumed in instalments over the next week or ten days, as rigorously as antibiotics or any other more orthodox medication.

My grandfather's energized ash was most effective, it was said, against poisonous insect bites and jaundice. One family tale went thus: When he was still living in New Delhi, working as a civil servant, my grandfather had as a visitor one of the most eminent physicists of the time. His scientific temper would, of course, not allow him to actually trust in such mumbo-jumbo, but his scientific temper was overruled by his wife's temper, which urged him in no uncertain terms to get his particularly severe jaundice treated by Ramachandran-mama.

So the scientist arrived, bursting with bad bile and disbelief. My grandfather began, his usual methods augmented for jaundice only by a shallow bowl of water set near his patient. As he traced and whispered, he would move his hand from the patient to the bowl, back to the patient and then back to the bowl. Slowly the water turned a sickly yellow-green.

'What's that?' the scientist barked.

'That's the excess bilirubin in you,' he was told.

'That can't be,' he shot back, and when the treatment ended, he whisked the bowl off with him, to be tested at a lab.

Being a family story, the denouement was naturally dramatic. The scientist came back the next day or the day after, fell at my grandfather's feet, and begged to be forgiven for his scepticism. The lab had found traces of bilirubin in the water. More importantly, he was feeling remarkably better already, his jaundice slowly inching towards the exit.

I never had jaundice, and I don't think any insects beyond the routine household menagerie of mosquitoes and ants ever bit me. But in my fierce attacks of childhood asthma, my grandfather's art met its match. Time and again, I would sit in front of him, wheezing and heaving, crumpled from lack of breath, while he concentrated ever harder and traced ever more purposefully. In my schoolbag, as regularly present as the lunch it accompanied, would be a neat newspaper sachet of *vibhuthi*, to be taken during breaks. I came to know its taste the way a caffeine addict knows his espresso.

But it did no good. An attack would wane, but the next dusty place, or the next change of season, or the next drink of cold water would set it flaring again. Secretly, and the fable of the sceptical scientist notwithstanding, I always wondered if it was because I just didn't believe hard enough—if, in faith healing, it was as important for the healed to have faith as for the healer.

Eventually, as I grew older, my asthma started to make only sporadic appearances, as if it had been worn out by my parents' infinite energy and their kitchen-sink approach to treatment. We tried, almost literally, everything—nebulisers and tablets, of course, but also yoga, exercise, homeopathy, variously controlled diets, an ice-cream-free existence, and Ayurveda. I ate boiled eggs for months on end because one doctor said it would help strengthen my constitution. Another time, I was told to perform the yogic trick of pouring warm salt water into one nostril, having it flush the respiratory passages, and return out of the other nostril. I was seven or eight years old, so unsurprisingly, I did it wrong and snorted myself full of the solution. Sometimes, during bumpy car rides or airplane turbulence, I imagine I can still feel the saline sloshing around inside my lungs.

The one thing I did not try, the one nostrum that seemed too exotic even for my parents, was the famous 'fish treatment' of Hyderabad, involving the wilful ingestion of a live murrel fingerling that had been stuffed to its gills with an unknown medicine. Perhaps because it was the sole remedy that we resisted, it took on the romance of untold promise; European colonists in Africa, training their gaze on the mysteries of the only unexplored continent, must have felt the same way.

But the fish treatment was also so visibly and glamorously an Event, far more than boiled eggs and nasal lavage. The bronchially disadvantaged would flock to Hyderabad every summer for this free treatment, often brought in from diverse corners of India on special trains run just for the purpose. As they queued patiently, they would appear on television news reports, which never seemed to tire of the spectacle. The crowds were estimated in the hundreds of thousands, and the medicine itself was said to date back to the mid-nineteenth century. The sheer scale of all this seemed, to my mind, to be entirely appropriate. After all, the treatment of something as elemental as asthma, which robs you of the very breath of life, should be epic and enigmatic and miraculously curative.

The history of this marathon of healing—or, at least, the history as explained by the Bathini Goud family, which keeps its proprietary treatment a closely held secret—dates back to 1845. In that year, the life of one Veeranna Goud changed dramatically. Till then, he had been a toddy tapper by caste and profession, but he was one of Andhra Pradesh's more philanthropic toddy tappers. 'He gave away a third of whatever he earned to the poor, no matter how much or how little it was,' Bathini Harinath Goud told me. 'That's just the type of man he was.'

When I met him, Harinath was sixty-eight and rake-thin, his

white beard matched by equally white, very fierce tufts of hair sprouting from his ears. He'd been participating in his family's annual ritual for sixty-three years. 'Veeranna Goud was my great-grandfather. He had one son, Shivram, who also had only one son, Shankar,' Harinath said. Shankar, though, was more prolific; he had five sons and four daughters. 'Between us, we've been conducting this treatment since our father passed away in 1962.'

In 1845, that annus mirabilis of Veeranna Goud, a sage from the Himalayas had descended into the plains and was wandering India. It was the start of the monsoon, and when Veeranna encountered him, the sage was wet, hungry and homeless. 'Veeranna fed and clothed him—expecting, of course, nothing in return,' Harinath said. 'The sage saw that he wouldn't commercialize this gift, that he would use it to help his fellow man. So he taught him the art of making this medicine.'

The recipe for this medicine has not left the Goud family since; in fact, even Goud daughters never learn it because, Harinath said, 'after all, when they get married, they go into another family.' All that's known is that it is a lumpy paste, in a vivid shade of yellow. The paste is rolled into a ball, stuffed into the mouth of a month-old, two-inch-long murrel fish, which is in turn stuffed into the waiting gullet of a patient, to be swallowed intact. 'As the fish wriggles on its way down, it helps disperse the medicine more effectively,' one pseudo-scientific argument in favour of the treatment goes, conveniently forgetting that asthma plagues the bronchial tubes, not the oesophagus.

Two days before Mrigashira Karthi—the day that signifies the advent of the monsoon every year, and the day on which the Gouds spend twenty-four straight hours thrusting fish down throats—Harinath's house in Hyderabad's Kawadiguda section was surprisingly peaceful. Cell phones were ringing more insistently than usual, there were stacks of pink and blue flyers on nearly every available surface, and squadrons of relatives, descended upon Hyderabad to help with the cure, paraded past us on their way in or out. But I'd expected secrecy and urgency, murmurs of incantations, perhaps even the odd sniff of brewing medicine—a Witches' Sabbath of activity. Instead, I had Harinath relaxing on a sofa, and two grandchildren, fresh out of their baths, anointing themselves liberally with Nycil talcum powder in front of a mirror.

Harinath handed me one of the flyers that would be distributed on the day of the treatment. In Telugu, English and Hindi, the flyers listed a strict diet, consisting of exactly twenty-seven items, which had to be followed for forty-five days after the treatment. It was an unusual menu. It included old rice and dried mango pieces but also goat meat; it recommended idlis but not chutney; it painstakingly listed, as individual items, even spices like turmeric, salt and pepper. Oddest of all was Item No. 27, which read like a bizarre chemistry experiment: 'Heat an iron rod. Soak it in cow's buttermilk and drink it.'

'And you have to take the medicine as well, every fifteen days during that forty-five-day period, in the form of little pellets,' Harinath said. 'And then come back for the fish treatment for the next two years.' Although these days, he added vaguely, because of all the fertilizer in the food and the pollution in the air, it could even take three or four years for the treatment to dig its feet in. At that, the bubble of my boyhood vision quivered violently. This sounded nothing like epic or enigmatic or miraculously curative. Why, it even had pellet-sized dosages of medicine! It may as well have been homeopathy!

⌒

As he spoke, Harinath exhibited a strange verbal tic that puzzled me at first. He talked easily and at length, in almost pre-crafted sentences, about his family's history, but every time he said the word 'dawai'—'treatment' or 'medicine'—he stumbled, caught himself, and replaced it with the word 'prasadam.' Selectively and specifically, he was bowdlerizing his own speech.

Behind that tic, I was to discover, lay a decade-long back-story of rising opposition in Hyderabad to the Goud fish treatment. The opposition has been led by two organizations—the Jana Vignana Vedika, an NGO that was born of, but no longer resides with, the Communist Party of India–Marxist; and the Hyderabad chapter of the America-based Center for Inquiry, a non-profit that promotes reason and science over superstition.

In the early 2000s, this opposition began to hotly question everything about the treatment—its efficacy, its secrecy, its potential for harm, and its promotion by the Andhra Pradesh government. When I met Harinath, it was a couple of weeks before a public-interest litigation came up for hearing in a Hyderabad city civil court, challenging five government departments and the Gouds. Two years earlier, in the face of such contention, the government had felt compelled to put up a banner at the treatment's venue, stating that the 'medicine' had no curative properties. 'Ha! That had no effect on attendance at all,' Harinath said, with a snort.

Innaiah Narisetti, a former journalist and the chair of the local Center for Inquiry chapter, is a dignified, articulate man, with a track record like the back of a porcupine, bristling with sharp needles of attack against irrational belief and superstition. 'This is a cult organization,' he said. 'The doctors say it isn't scientific. It isn't hygienic. No patient records are maintained; there are no follow-up visits. But still they claim a cure! That is bogus.' I mentioned to him Harinath's tic, of labelling it a 'prasadam' instead of a cure, and Narisetti laughed. 'The courts won't get taken in by that. They'll see through it, they'll see that it's just a strategy.'

Part of Narisetti's harangue included the understandable grievances of the wronged taxpayer. Until 1997, the Gouds had conducted their event, at their own expense, in their ancestral home in the old Doodh Bowli quarter of Hyderabad. 'People would sleep in the alleys near our house, on the sidewalk, just for this,' Harinath remembered. 'You'd get tears in your eyes just listening to them cough all night.' In 1997, though, following some communal turmoil, a curfew was imposed in Doodh Bowli. N. Chandrababu Naidu, then chief minister of Andhra Pradesh, started to allow the Gouds free use of larger public spaces—for a year, the Nizam College's football fields, and subsequently the Exhibition Grounds in Nampally, its new home.

Eleven years later, when I attended, there was even more evidence of government support—eight ambulances, 1,100 police personnel, six closed-circuit televisions, and an assured power supply of 1,000 kilowatts. Navin Mittal, the district collector, did some rough mental arithmetic and told me that the government would spend roughly Rs 60 lakhs of taxpayer money in manpower and resources for the event. Which only proves that Milton Friedman was right: There is no such thing as a free lunch, or even a free snack of nutritious murrel fish.

But that's not all, Narisetti hastened to point out. 'There are huge losses because the state supplies the fish as well, selling them to the crowds for Rs 10 each,' he said. 'All these fish are ordered, but word has spread that this treatment is not working, so the crowds have come down. Last year, there were thousands of wasted fish.'

But, I feebly ventured, my boyhood bubble quivering some more, 'Harinath said there were four lakh attendees last year?'

'Not at all,' Narisetti said. 'There were twenty thousand.'

The next morning, I hunted down the Department of Fisheries to clarify this number. V. Raghothama Swamy, the joint director there, was in the midst of aggregating, from various ponds and tanks in Andhra Pradesh, thousands of murrel fingerlings, remotely monitoring their journeys to Hyderabad like an anxious chaperone.

'So how many fish, exactly, did you distribute last year?' I asked.

'Forty-five thousand,' Swamy said.

Again, I mentioned Goud's figure of four lakh attendees to him. He smiled indulgently, glanced at a colleague, and then said, as if softening the blow to a child who'd discovered that Santa Claus was fictional. 'Well, there were also ten thousand or so vegetarians and they take their medicine in jaggery. And many attendants for the asthmatics were also present, you must remember. So the crowd was large.'

'But was it four lakhs?'

'No. Definitely not,' Swamy answered.

On my way down the stairs, I saw a poster hanging on the wall. It showed many fish, lying quite dead in a net, being pulled in from the ocean. The caption read: 'Fish is our health.' Suddenly, I wasn't so sure.

The bleeding taxpayers aside, the other prong of the opposition to the Goud treatment attacks the medicine itself, the yellow paste that the family claims is concocted on the principles of Ayurveda. A few years earlier, the Gouds had sent samples of the paste to the Central Drug Research Institute in Lucknow and to the Indian Institute of Chemical Biology in Kolkata. The latter's report, which Harinath photocopied and handed to me, refused to offer any opinions about the paste's curative abilities. It would only offer, grudgingly, that the paste wouldn't actually kill you—because an assay revealed heavy metal concentrations to be within the limits prescribed by law—and that it had no steroids secretly working against the asthma.

Harinath also had another letter, which, mystifyingly, he freely showed me. It was from the Department of Ayurveda,

Yoga and naturopathy, Unani, Siddha and Homoeopathy, or AYUSH, a government body that purports to govern such alternative medicine. The AYUSH letter refused to classify the Gouds' cure as Ayurveda, calling it 'at best . . . a folklore medicine practised by a traditional healer, who is not institutionally qualified.'

The thing with conviction, of course, is that it can operate to extreme lengths on the side of both belief and disbelief. Harinath, in his quest to persuade me of his paste's medicinal properties, allowed himself to be swept into a current of questionable rhetoric. 'We have test-tube babies now, so why don't we believe the legend of Duryodhana and his brothers being born of a ball of flesh?' he asked. 'We have rocket ships now, so why not the *vimanas* of the Ramayana?'

Narisetti, the advocate of rationalism, is no less vulnerable to making flatly provocative statements. 'The government should be supporting only culture, not religion. Religion is a superstitious belief. It is not a part of culture,' he told me. But religion, and particularly in India, informs so much of our culture, I offered—the food we eat, the clothes we wear, the festivals we celebrate, the classical music we listen to, the art and theatre we support. 'That can all survive without religion,' he said. And then, a step further: 'The government's job is to educate people about this, to show that religion is just a superstitious belief. The government should reduce the presence of religion gradually until we finally get rid of it. That's when we will live in a really secular society.'

The two men, in a sense, were funhouse mirror versions of each other—Harinath with his faith, and Narisetti with his faith in the sheer irrelevance of faith. But somehow, to believe as deeply as Harinath seemed to believe, even in something as unfounded as his asthma remedy, jarred me less than Narisetti's dismissal of religion altogether. For the first time in my life, I felt more unsettled by the views of the faithless than by the views of the faithful.

〜

Even if the entire event was a manufactured sham (as opposed to an unconscious sham, and in the intent to dupe lies a vast difference), nobody could tell me exactly what purpose such a sham would serve. One argument had it that the Goud community formed an important vote bank in Andhra Pradesh, and that politicians preferred to support the Bathini Goud family rather than offend the community's sentiment. But more puzzling still was the Gouds' own motivation to do this every year, for no remuneration—to prepare their paste, to stand at the head of a throbbing crowd, in the stifling heat that throbbing crowds effortlessly throw off, and stick their hands down dozens of unfamiliar throats every hour. As a mere hobby, that sounds—and is—severely overrated.

Eager theories account for this too. A few years ago, in a significant windfall, the Chandrababu Naidu government was said to have handed over to the Gouds some land in Old Hyderabad. 'They said it was to grow their herbs,' Narisetti said. 'Till then, they claimed they were sourcing the herbs from the Himalayas, and that the land would make their task easier.' Also, Narisetti added, the Gouds get a cut from the auxiliary businesses that spring up around the centrepiece event every year—shops of toys and clothes, food stalls, pushcarts of religious paraphernalia, all selling to the captive audience at the Exhibition Grounds.

It all sounded just about plausible; there have been more improbably painstaking moneymaking schemes than the caper thus outlined. And yet, the day before the treatment, when Harinath walked into the little office at the Exhibition Grounds, he didn't head directly to the young girl who was seated behind a desk handing out advance tokens; he didn't ask to know how many tokens had been distributed or what the response was. Instead, he strode very rapidly into the office, straight to waist-high stacks of fresh flyers that had just been delivered there, still warm from the printers. He peeled away a flyer from the top and scanned the instructions and the list of twenty-seven permitted items on the diet sheet. Then he relaxed, smiled, and said to his companion: 'It's all there, it's all correct.' To me, that didn't seem like the behaviour of a man out to skim a few rupees off the sale of every cheap plastic whistle or multicoloured T-shirt.

The Doodh Bowli section of Hyderabad, lying a couple of kilometres from the Charminar, is an ancient quarter of mosques and thin, confusing streets that regularly double back upon themselves. The Bathini Goud family's ancestral home, tucked into one of these streets, had been newly whitewashed, and its parrot-green window frames had been repainted. 'We do a pooja the day before, at the house in Doodh Bowli. It's usually just the family, but you must come,' Harinath had said, and so I had gone, curious to see the clan.

By the time Harinath and I arrived, the family was already assembled on the terrace, under a temporary canopy of cloth. In a corner, next to a small altar, the family priest sat murmuring to himself and glaring occasionally at the world at large. Harinath whipped off his shirt and sat down in the front, next to his two older brothers. I took a discreet seat at the back, feeling slightly self-conscious until I saw my fellow intruder—a French documentary filmmaker with a digital video camera, who orbited the congregation like a diligent planet, filming the entire pooja.

Truth to tell, there wasn't much to film. This was a regular Satyanarayana pooja, performed in many Hindu homes before an occasion of significance. And like almost every one of the

The Bathini Goud Brothers; Harinath sits second from left

communal poojas I've ever attended, there were the requisite distracted children, the whimpering baby, the sombre gentlemen up front, and the comforting white noise of women talking and laughing at the back. Harinath, sweating even in spite of the playful surges of monsoonal breeze that cut through the midday heat, sat very still, eyes closed, hands folded in prayer.

We must have sat there for at least an hour in this manner, and attentions began to flag. The filmmaker filmed from less bravura angles, the baby whimpered louder, Harinath sweated more, and the children, losing patience, began to make sorties downstairs into the cooler confines of the house. A little while later, some men began to bring up huge wicker baskets of cooked rice, sweets and pooris, and steel buckets of sambar and rasam. In the heat, and in the restricted confines of the canopy, the wonderful, dense smell of the food rose and hung, like a spice-seeded storm cloud, above the family. Attentions, unsurprisingly, wilted further.

Harinath finally broke a coconut, a girl came and tied a red-and-yellow thread, with a betel leaf, around the wrists of us observers, and the priest performed his *arati*, offering up cubes of sugar and diced bananas to the deity. It seemed like the end, but then the group moved downstairs, first to the house's stuffy pooja room and then to the real focus of all this consecration: the well.

When we'd first met, I had asked Harinath whether he had ever considered taking his treatment across India, like a travelling apothecary. He had bridled at the suggestion and then said, cryptically: 'We need our Doodh Bowli well.' Later I had persuaded him to explain that statement, and he told me about the importance of making the medicine with the water from the well in the Doodh Bowli house. 'Only that water. Nothing else will do,' he had said. One summer, he claimed, every well in Doodh Bowli had gone dry, and Hyderabad had thirsted for water—yet the well in the ancestral home had gushed with sweet, cool water.

That well is really a small, square hole in the ground, set to one side of the courtyard past the entrance of the house. Just above it, built into the staircase leading to the terrace, is a sacred *tulasi* plant in a bower, as if it were benignly conferring its holy status upon the well all year round. The water is not too far below the surface, but it remains so cool that even leaning over it, during the summer months, feels like passing through a blast of air conditioning.

The priest now took position over the well and consecrated it with rice, vermillion and turmeric. As if he were a trainer pepping his boxer for the big fight, the priest flattered the well water in his recitations, calling it the embodiment of the Ganga, the Yamuna, the Narmada, the Kaveri and the Sindhu rivers. In the pooja room behind us, the women had gathered independently and were singing in low, tuneless voices. Only after that was it time to eat.

After lunch, the Bathini Goud residence was flooded with visitors—neighbours dropping in to see how things were going, more members of the family, reporters and camera crews to interview Harinath, who seemed to have been designated communications director for the event. His daughter Alka took charge of his two cell phones, answering some calls and giving others to her father. It was, by now, past three in the afternoon, and I asked Harinath: 'But when will you actually begin making the medicine?'

'We'll probably start in the evening, or later at night, when all this has died down.'

I thought about that, and then asked: 'Can I stay to watch?'

Harinath smiled a slow, sweet smile, and said: 'You know that isn't possible.'

I knew. I'd just figured that there was no harm in trying.

With little to do until the start of the treatment the next evening, I wandered back to the Exhibition Grounds and sat in the little office building, near the Bartronics desk. Bartronics, a Hyderabad-based company, had installed automated entry systems into other locations with teeming crowds, such as the Vaishno Devi shrine in the Himalayas and the Tirumala temple at Tirupathi. The previous year, Bartronics had been engaged to implement a similar process at the Exhibition Grounds, and with needless zeal, a sophisticated biometrics system, involving fingerprints and photographs, was installed.

'But it began to take a long time to check the biometrics, and people started shouting and complaining,' a Bartronics employee told me. 'Besides, there's no real danger of any malpractice here, since it's all free.' So biometrics sat it out on the bench this year. Instead, people came to the office two or three days in advance to pick up two tokens—one for the fish counter, and one that allotted them to a specific, one-hour window of time. Then they walked away planning to come early anyway. 'You know, just in case,' one man said.

Sitting next to the token-dispensing desk, I began to detect, in Harinath's prospective patients, the same hesitant hope that I'd seen in my grandfather's visitors many years ago. A number of them asked: 'Does this really work?' and the beleaguered Bartronics lady was forced to say that she was just giving out the tokens. Some scrutinized the token intently, as if it held some clue to their prospects. A few hung around, after they'd pocketed their tokens, to look at the others who came after them, as if the appearance of their fellow ward-mates would give them a better idea of this unorthodox hospital.

One middle-aged man had flown from Montreal to be at Hyderabad during the treatment. 'My lungs operate at about 38 per cent capacity. I have to travel with a bag full of medication,' he said, showing me a plastic pouch crammed with tablets, nebulisers, capsules and a syringe. He looked in the bloom of health, but he said he'd spent his life trying medications of various provenances. 'I can't even travel alone; I need a friend with me all the time.' He'd read about the Bathini Goud remedy on the internet. 'Right about now, I'm willing to try anything.'

Amarendra Kumar, an automobile dealer from Bihar, came with his wife, both looking to be able to breathe freely again. He had arrived in Hyderabad the previous morning, mistakenly believing that the treatment would start the day I met them. 'I had booked my return tickets for tomorrow afternoon's train,' he said, worried. 'Now I'll have to cancel and rebook for Sunday.'

The most uncertain visitors of the afternoon were a Jain family of four. They entered together and stood next to me, silently watching the tokens change hands. Then the father tapped me on the shoulder and asked: 'Does it work better with the fish?'

'It's supposed to,' I told him. 'There's a vegetarian version, but the fish is said to be more effective.'

He stepped back into a moment's silence and then said, almost to himself: 'But we don't eat meat.'

More silence, and then, sensing that the family was not quite as well informed as they should have been, I said: 'You do know that the fish is alive, don't you?'

This ignited a conflagration of comical reactions. The father sank deeper into worry. The mother, though, laughed almost hysterically. She then walked resolutely to the door and started to mock-retch graphically, holding her stomach, a mischievous smile playing over her face. 'Come on,' she'd say between heaves, 'no fish, let's go.' Her older son, aged approximately ten, looked fascinated by the newly gruesome lustre to this treatment. His younger brother, who must have been six or seven, tugged at his father's shirt, pulling him away, his face crumpling slowly in horror like a sheet of cellophane.

The father wrestled with himself for five whole minutes. Then he stepped up to the Bartronics counter and asked for two tokens for his children. 'Only in case the fish is needed,' he justified to his family. But if the quest for his sons' perfect health did win out over the tenets of his religion, who could blame him?

Saturday evening proved to be hot, sticky and humid, the sort of weather that prompts the imagination to believe that moisture can simply be wrung out of the air. Hyderabad's traffic, re-routed near Nampally to keep the approach to the Exhibition Grounds clear, was at its thorniest best. I entered the Grounds at half past eight for a treatment that was supposed to have begun an hour earlier. But I needn't have worried. The Bathini Gouds, leaving Doodh Bowli with their vats of medicine, travelling under police escort, had reached the venue only at eight o'clock, snared in the traffic rearrangements organized for their benefit.

By the time I arrived, the little road leading to the Grounds' Ajanta Gate was clogged with people, flanked on either side by what Narisetti had called the 'auxiliary businesses.' Spread out on tarpaulins on the ground or on rickety pushcarts were T-shirts, children's shoes, toys with crazy lights and wailing sounds, and bags in cloth and plastic. Nothing, as far as I asked, was priced at more than Rs 20, and the vendors, instead of looking excited at the prospect of a twenty-four-hour sales extravaganza, were following with forlorn eyes the crowds that rushed past them.

By 5 p.m. on that day, the Bartronics people had told me, around thirty-five thousand advance tokens had been given out, but the entrance into the Grounds was surprisingly serene. On low, broad concrete platforms, people squatted, ate, slept and played, patiently waiting for the time slot printed on their tickets. On the public address system, between bursts of shehnai music, an announcer, already hoarse, was warning people not to pinch their plastic bags of fish close. 'The fish will suffocate. Keep the mouth of the bag open.' And then again the same announcement followed in Hindi and Telugu.

Walking past police and medical assistance booths, stalls for free food, stalls for water, and a slumbering fire engine, I entered the maze that led up to the dais. Under a temporary tin roof, these passages, formed by iron railings and rickety wooden staves, were designed to direct the crowds to one of thirty-three counters up front; they reminded me of immigration queues at large international airports. The token system may have mitigated the crowd within those passages, but it could do nothing about the way everybody pressed up densely near the counters. Two-thirds of the maze was empty, but near every one of the thirty-three counters, people clamoured to go first, holding up their little bags of fish like cigarette lighters at a rock concert.

Pushing my way through the stifling heat of this mosh pit and squeezing out with a pop at the front, I found Harinath, in his yellow shawl and white dhoti, in an oasis of relative calm. 'At my age,' he said, 'I can't stand at those counters and work at that pace.' The others worked faster, often pushing fish into five or six mouths per minute, standing in a crowd and unaware or uncaring of the growing pools of muddy water around their feet. Harinath, for his part, positioned himself one rank behind the rest of his family, near a little raised stage area where he could occasionally sit and contemplate the ocean of people in front of him.

An old matriarch of Harinath's family, sitting behind him and rolling out miniature cannonballs of medicine, handed me one. It was a livid yellow from the turmeric, but it smelled and tasted of almost pure asafoetida, a spice whose very root is the word 'foetid.' I have not been able to stomach the taste of asafoetida ever since, at a very young age, I mistook a hunk of it in my upma for a peanut, bit eagerly into it, and proceeded to throw up violently. I rolled that lump of medicine around in my fingers only for a few seconds, but I could still smell the asafoetida the next morning.

As soon as I reached Harinath, he began collaring familiar faces from the crowd and bringing them over to make introductions. 'This woman, she's come from Maharashtra two times already, and her asthma is much better,' he would say. 'Go on! Tell him how much better your asthma is.'

'Much better,' the woman said sincerely.

'See, she's much better,' Harinath beamed.

Even aside from these testimonies for my benefit, people would rush up to Harinath to thank him, or to even just touch him, as if that were supplementary blessing. One man with a withered leg somehow jettisoned his crutches to kneel and touch Harinath's feet. Others would tell him, like children proudly reporting their mathematics scores to their parents, that they were '75 per cent better' or even '98 per cent better,' as if they were able to keenly calibrate even a 2 per cent remainder of their asthma.

But the unmistakable soundtrack to the Bathini Goud marathon cure was that of crying and retching. The cure was hardest on the young—the young fish, of course, but also the young children. Parents would lift their children bodily, holding them and keeping their mouths open. Harinath would slip the murrel fish out of its plastic sac, pinch its neck to open its mouth, and insert a dose of medicine. Then, with two long and dextrous fingers, he would stick the fish all the way at the back of the throat, snap the child's jaw shut, and squeeze the nose, forcing the child to gulp and swallow.

Not surprisingly, the results were often disastrous. One girl, who must have been twelve or thirteen, attempted to throw up as soon as she was let go; her father, equally adamant, tried to force her mouth shut. Other children, even young infants, swallowed their fish perfectly, but they instantly began wailing in horror, as if instinct, or the enforced feel of the whole exercise, had told them that something unnatural had just happened. One boy shouted in alarm: 'It's in my throat, ma, I can still feel it!' His mother began rubbing down his gullet, hoping to encourage the fish to complete the journey to its doom.

The adults didn't always fare better. Many, it is true, took approximately two seconds to swallow and move on. In a feat of physiological control, one composed gentleman was even able to indicate, to his minder, that his fish had gone down the wrong length of piping, bring it back up into his mouth, and then swiftly re-ingest it. But one woman, with the fish in her throat, thumped herself on her chest and brought it back out. Harinath picked it up off the coir matting on the floor, checked if it was still alive, swirled it around in a bucket of chlorine water, and tried again.

And then, suddenly, it was my turn.

The most disconcerting moment of the entire process was a few seconds of stasis, when Harinath held the fish up, medicine gleaming in its mouth, and I stood with my mouth open as if it were the Eucharist wafer, dimly aware that I could still twist away and run. Then the stasis broke, and Harinath's hand, full of fish, was in my mouth.

From all the first-hand observation that evening, I must have somehow learned how to swallow right, because the fish went down, tail first, much easier than I expected. It was slippery and small, and although I felt an initial tickle, I think it had expired by the time it was a third of the way down my throat. Right away, though, I realized that it wasn't the fish that was making people retch; it was the asafoetida, so strong and vicious that tears started in your eyes in that very first second. Then, as it slid down, it burned such a trail of further pungency down your throat that your hair stood on end and your fingers clenched involuntarily. Eyes still streaming, I grabbed at a bottle of water behind Harinath, although somehow, my mind had inscrutably fixed on its own preferred solution to the asafoetida's pungency: fresh-cut mangoes.

For a few further hours into the night, I sat behind Harinath and watched the crowds. I watched many, many people come right up to Harinath, their nerve screwed up, fully aware of what lay before them—and then they backed out, hope and false courage defeated by the immediate reality. As they walked away, they seemed puzzled and distressed, not so much by what they'd narrowly avoided as by their sudden loss of faith. It was almost as if they had desperately wanted to believe but had been finally let down by their closest accomplice: their own body.

I watched Harinath too. He rested only in snatches of a few minutes, and he was almost always talking and enquiring and blessing. Not for the first time, I wondered what was in it for him—whether it was the sense that, at least for one day every year, the Bathini Gouds were the most important and influential people in Hyderabad. Whether it was that their fish 'remedy'—remedy or not—defined them, gave them an identity. Whether there was some hidden commercial motive, or whether the Gouds really believed that they were sending people home asthma-free. Really, there was no way to tell. But for a few moments, watching Harinath at work, I was reminded powerfully of my grandfather and his healing sessions, of his roaring faith, and of how, in that charged slice of time, for both the healer and the healed—and even for me, watching with a child's easily suspended disbelief—anything was possible. We could all be well again.

3
On the ear lobe that changed history

In Manapadu, on the southern coast of Tamil Nadu, some imaginative soul has enlivened the uphill walk to the Church of the Holy Cross by installing reminders of Christ's parallel struggle up the hill of Calvary. Every few metres, there are little plaster-of-Paris dioramas of the various stages of that journey: Here of Christ first shouldering the cross, there of Him stumbling under its weight, and further on of Veronica offering her veil to wipe His perspiration away. The series may well have been commissioned by a sly church elder, as if to challenge his lazier parishioners by saying: 'You complain about this stroll uphill? Think of the trek your Lord undertook for you!' But if that was the case, the dioramas are unnecessary, for not only is the slope gentle and forgiving on the ankles, but the Church of the Holy Cross is also irresistibly attractive—worthy, in fact, of a much steeper hill.

On the December morning I visited, the wind hurried strongly off the sea, careening around the top of the hill in mad eddies, shrieking around the corners of buildings. The sun was not hot but bright, and it was impossible to look without squinting at the brilliantly whitewashed walls of the church. The sea resembled a vast stretch of aluminium foil, slowly folding and unfolding itself. Standing near the church's northern wall, I could see Manapadu's perfect natural harbour, a long, sandy crescent of coast, with fishing boats pulled up the beach in ragged lines, and the water so shallow that the dirty brown of the seabed showed through the shining water. It was the Monday before Christmas, and I thought I was the only one there.

The Church of the Holy Cross is a plain white building, trimmed in deep blue, a very Mediterranean-looking sort of structure. They say it holds a relic—a sliver of the true cross— that was brought to Manapadu in processional pomp from Cochin, over eight months in 1583. The sliver was, unfortunately, not on display, and I'm not sure it ever is. In front of the altar, an old woman sat with her hands clasped, praying noiselessly; if it hadn't been for me, she would have had the small church entirely to herself. Near the giant cross in the apse, an old Bible stood open on a trestle table, its pages looking weary from use; on either side of the apse, blue windows creaked and groaned, buffeted by the wind. Despite that racket, and despite the ceaseless slap of the waves on the coast, I remember the church as being quiet. It can't have been, of course, but memory often confuses tranquillity with silence.

At this church, a rusted metal signboard will tell you, St. Francis Xavier offered Mass in 1542, his first on the eastern shores of India. He had arrived by sea from the opposite coast, hugging the southern Indian peninsula and making frequent stops all along. At Manapadu, he landed and, for reasons known only to himself, took up residence for some weeks in a cave. The cave still exists, a short walk down a sandy path leading from the church to the sea, past a newer and smaller shrine to the saint, on the rocky lip of the coast. There, a sign reads:

*This cave (once the dwelling of a Saivite sanyasi) has been
sanctified by the prayers and penances of St. Francis Xavier.*

As grottoes by the sea go, this one seemed remarkably
unnatural, having been augmented at some point by wooden
ceiling beams, square pillars hewn out of rock, blue paint on the
walls, and a wooden lintel under the arched doorway. At the cave's
deepest point, against its back wall, there was a small statue of
Xavier and a Mirinda bottle half-full of oil for the two lamps.
To the right, just inside the entrance, was a shallow well, fed
allegedly by the ocean just outside. 'It's true—you put a lemon
into the well, and it will wash out into the sea a few minutes
later,' I was told by many people. (Oddly, in every version of the
test that I heard, it was always a lemon, as if the use of a banana
or a tin can would be like using something other than litmus to
settle the acid–alkali confusion.) The 'miracle' of the well is that,
despite its connection to the sea, the water is supposed to taste
sweet and fresh. I drank half a cup, out of a pail standing near
the well, and while the water tasted faintly brackish, it certainly
wasn't half a cup of seawater.

The Church of the Holy Cross was here when Francis Xavier
moved into his cave. In the 1530s, a Portuguese trading ship called
the *Santiago* foundered near Manapadu, and its mast washed
up on the beach. 'But somebody accidentally stepped on it, and
a terrible thing happened,' Valentin Ilango, a high school Tamil
teacher and a passionate historian of Manapadu, told me with
dramatically rolling eyes. We were sitting in his staffroom, the
school cloaked in the anxious hush of examinations. 'This man
became gravely ill, and his body swelled up. Then the captain of
the ship had a dream that the mast was to be erected as a cross,
and that it was to be washed and oiled. When the captain did
that, in 1540, the poor man recovered.' By 1582, a church had
grown up around that original mast, which remains now as the

spine of a bigger, newer cross. It is still washed and oiled on feast days.

Xavier arrived here a couple of years after the mast became a cross. 'He lived in that cave, and he prayed all night. If he ate at all, it was only one meal a day, and he would eat the food that the local fisher folk brought him—rice gruel, dried fish, things like that,' Ilango said. 'From the cave, he wrote, I think, twelve letters to St. Ignatius of Loyola, which are said to be in the Vatican's library in Rome.' When Xavier finally emerged, he set off for Tuticorin, on the project that had brought him to these parts: Cementing the conversion to Catholicism of the fishing community in the area.

In a chapter in Jules Verne's *20,000 Leagues Under the Sea*, the narrator, M. Aronnax, is watching Captain Nemo fondle a gigantic, perfect pearl when he sees a shadow in the water. He fears it is a shark but, as he writes, it is only a man:

> . . . *a living man, an Indian, a fisherman, a poor devil who, I suppose, had come to glean before the harvest. I could see the bottom of his canoe anchored some feet above his head. He dived and went up successively. A stone held between his feet, cut in the shape of a sugar loaf, while a rope fastened him to his boat, helped him to descend more rapidly. This was all his apparatus. Reaching the bottom about five yards deep, he went on his knees and filled his bag with oysters picked up at random. Then he went up, emptied it, pulled up his stone, and began the operation once more, which lasted thirty seconds.*

The *Nautilus*, at the time, was lurking off the final sandy curve of India's east coast, which makes Aronnax's Indian, in all probability, a member of the pearl-fishing community living between Rameshwaram and Kanyakumari, concentrated in particular in Tuticorin and its neighbouring villages. The fishermen may date themselves back to antiquity, but there is still debate, academic as well as popular, about their very nomenclature. Tamil Sangam literature, from the years between 300 BCE and 200 CE, refers to them as 'neithalimakkal,' or 'people of the coastal tracts,' but this seems too poetically generic. For long, the fishermen were known by their caste—Parava—but many today prefer to be called Bharathas or Bharathakulas, which instantly confers a martial lineage dating back to Bharatha, king of Ayodhya and brother of Rama. Another, rather more extreme theory believes the Paravas to be one of the lost tribes of Israel. But Hindu or Jewish roots notwithstanding, they are now almost overwhelmingly Catholic—and that happened because of one man's ear lobe.

Early in the sixteenth century, a seaman of the Kayalar caste—which had been recently converted to Islam by Arab traders—insulted a Parava woman with an epithet that is unfortunately lost to history. Her husband, when he tried to intervene, got his ear lobe cut off for his troubles, losing his pearl earring in the bargain. With the Ear Lobe Incident, the long-simmering tensions between the Paravas and the Kayalar Muslims appear to have boiled over. The Paravas approached the newly arrived Portuguese for protection, and they were promised this in return for their faith and a monopoly on pearl fishing rights. So, in a mass baptism in the mid-1530s, roughly twenty thousand people from thirty villages converted to Christianity—possibly the biggest such single conversion in history. This was a conversion merely in the most elementary sense of the word: In her book titled *Saints, Goddesses and Kings*, in a chapter on the Paravas, Susan Bayly contends that it only involved 'being taught to make the sign of the cross and to recite garbled Tamil renderings of the creed and the Ave Maria.' For all its simplicity, nearly half a millennium later, the conversion seems to have held fast, at least on its surface.

The heart of Parava Catholicism is the Church of Our Lady of the Snows, on South Beach Road in Tuticorin. Locally called the Periya Kovil, or the Big Church, it is located down the road from the old harbour, where in the bygone days barrels of drinking water would be imported from Sri Lanka, and from where cargo still leaves for the Maldives. Across the road from the church is a slim cross, so evidently a converted mast that it is still festooned with nautical-looking bunting. (The cross-mast is, I would observe, a common, vivid symbol of the twinning of the Church and the fishing community in this area, as is an altar centrepiece at another of Tuticorin's churches: a large, open oyster bearing a creamy exaggeration of a pearl.) A few doors from the Church of Our Lady of the Snows was a blue, half-timbered structure, bearing a painted sign saying 'Justin Photo Colour Lab' and depicting a wild-eyed child presumably in the throes of being photographed. The sign looked as worn as the building it was labeling. 'That used to be the Pandiyapathi's house,' my friend Amalraaj Fernando said as we passed it on his motorcycle. 'I'll explain later.'

The Church of Our Lady of the Snows is, like so many local churches inspired by the Portuguese, painted in white and bright blue. It was consecrated, a signboard reads, in August 1582, but to my eyes, the church looked barely two hundred years old. (In 1707, the signboard mentions incidentally, the church 'saved miraculously' the town and surrounding villages from a heavy thunderbolt—from, in other words, a very loud sound.) To the tail of the older, more compact, central hall of the church, a new, rectangular room has been tacked on. In its sterile whiteness, this space could pass for a hospital waiting room if the altar weren't visible through the doors at one end. 'It was freshly painted for Christmas—that's why it looks the way it does,' Fernando told me.

A small, neat man, Fernando nominally runs a mobile recharge shop in Tuticorin but, to the dismay of his wife, spends more time cultivating his earnest interest in the town's history and in getting to know, nearly literally, everyone. On that first visit to the Periya Kovil, he talked in considerable detail, off the top of his head, about Mary of the Snows. 'In the fourth century, Rome was going through a severe drought—and yet, on the Esquiline Hill, it snowed,' Fernando said. 'Mary appeared in a dream to the Pope Liberius, at the time, directing him to build a church on that hill. That is now the Basilica of Santa Maria Maggiore.' The gilded statue of Mary in Our Lady of the Snows, flanked by miscellaneous putti, was a legendary one, Fernando added, brought to Tuticorin from Manila in the sixteenth century.

On a Sunday morning, three days before Christmas, I attended my first two Masses at Our Lady of the Snows. Up front, women sat on the floor with their children; behind them, in the few pews available, were the men and senior citizens. Some of the women sported fine, sheer, Iberian veils, worn on their heads like long conical caps, looking like they had stepped out of the canvas of a Velasquez painting. The men held handkerchiefs and absently swatted at flies, which in Tuticorin come in such XXL sizes that they rivalled the length of my thumb. A faint breeze blew across the church, bearing the distant voices of the harmless, Santa-hatted motorcycle gangs, shouting 'Merry Christmas' to passers-by as they sped through the road outside.

I did not follow the Tamil Mass too closely. The service was led by a junior priest with the trudging, uniform intonations of a university lecturer, and his sermon—on compassion, if I recall rightly—was dry and flaccid. He had positioned himself in front of a standing fan, and sporadically, his purple vestments would fly up from his white cassock, like the plumage of an exotic bird shaking itself dry. Next to me, on the floor, a little girl with liquid eyes tumbled into giggles every time this happened. From the balcony above me, a choir occasionally gave us music, accompanied by a keyboard that reeled off disco rhythms in step with the hymns.

The next Mass, in English, was delivered by Father Jerosin Kattar, the rector and parish priest of Our Lady of the Snows and a fireball of a speaker. To a thinner but more attentive crowd, he spoke about Christ's love for his subjects, equating it to an almost maternal love, of the sort embodied by the Virgin Mary. Kattar is a short man, in danger of being hidden by his pulpit, but he makes up for it with his resonant voice and his animated manner of speech. He posed rhetorical questions to his congregation, answered them most satisfactorily himself, plucked Biblical quotes out of the ether to support his answers, and drew conclusions that appeared watertight and irrefutable. During his predecessor's sermon, there was always a low vibrato of surreptitious conversation in the church; during Kattar's, his audience clung to his every word.

Kattar is a heavy-set man in his fifties, with broad, thick hands, gray hair combed neatly back from his forehead, and a dusting of white stubble; over his cassock of dulled white, around his midriff, a red sash sat comfortably. When I met him, he was on a five-year rotation in Tuticorin, occupying an office in the compound of Our Lady of the Snows. He carried a Tamil Bible in a zippered case of soft felt, and a mobile phone that rang to the strain of 'Hark now hear, the angels sing,' although that may have been a purely seasonal choice. 'I was in Rome just before this, for a two-year stint, but I didn't like it. It was far too bureaucratic,' he told me. 'I was itching to get back here, where I felt more involved with the community.'

Kattar converses as he preaches—with considered pauses, sentences modulated to a flourish, didactic patience, and a vivid sense of history. When, during one of our discussions, the subject of that Sunday morning Mass on maternal love came up, he rapidly traced its roots back to the days of the Portuguese conversion. 'Before Christianity arrived, the fishermen here used to worship Meenakshi or Bhagavathi Amman, and Xavier knew they were attached to their feminine goddesses,' Kattar said. 'That was why he emphasised the role of Mary rather than Christ—for one maternal goddess to take the place of another.' Even more animist beliefs, such as a near-superstitious regard for deities of the ocean, were subsumed by the Virgin; today, the Paravas of Tuticorin often call her their *Kadal Maatha*, or mother of the sea.

'The Paravas are very religious folks,' Kattar said. 'As people dealing on such a daily basis with nature, with their very life at stake, they develop great respect and confidence for the supernatural, for the power that has created the sea.' Kattar is a Parava himself, and perhaps that emboldened him to speak bluntly of his community—so bluntly that, at times, I caught tiny whiffs of a dismissive superiority. 'The fishing community is conditioned by its work and its situation—they're like a tribal people,' he once said. 'They have changed very little in six hundred years. Till recently, many of them were illiterate, and procreation was their only recreation.'

Then he softened. 'I think, essentially, you have to understand them to serve them, and many bishops and fathers before me didn't understand them,' he said. 'For instance, many of the fishermen talk loudly, because they are used to shouting over the sound of the wind and the waves. But that can be misunderstood as shouting.' There were problems of alcoholism and a persistent addiction to betel nut, Kattar admitted, but there were also many poets and musicians within the community, 'all originals.' 'They're very intelligent, very methodical,' he said, indulging in a too-sweeping anthropological generalization. 'You should see them in the villages, resolving a dispute or an argument. They weigh the pros and cons, and they arrive at a really measured way of according culpability.'

It was over the course of my conversations with Kattar that I learned how the Catholicism here resembled a veneer, applied upon an older base of Hindu customs and caste traditions, many of which the Church had wisely allowed to bubble up to the surface. There is syncretism in language, in how words such as 'kovil' and 'aradhana,' traditionally intended for temples and Hindu celebrations of worship, are now applied to churches and Catholic feasts. There is syncretism in practice, in the lighting of oil lamps instead of candles, in the full-stretch prostrations that men performed at Our Lady of the Snows, in conducting both the Hindu *valakappu* ceremony for pregnant women and Christian baptism for newborn babies, even in the respectful act of leaving one's shoes outside the entrance of the church. And sometimes, there is syncretism in thought, in how a Christian fisherman still propitiates the Hindu god Murugan and refers to him '*Machaan*' or 'Brother-in-law,' because Murugan's wife Valli came from Parava stock—at least according to a Parava legend that has somehow been comfortably ensconced within another faith for five hundred years now.

That Sunday morning, after Kattar's English Mass, Fernando took me to the smaller Sacred Heart Church, in a narrow road behind Our Lady of the Snows. The Sacred Heart functions more as a prayer hall than a church, and it was deserted at the time. But in a large blue-and-white shed next to it was another symbol of Parava syncretism: the Pon Ther, or the golden carriage. Since 1806, first annually and then every twelve years and now every five years, the idol of Our Lady of the Snows is installed in the Ther, which is then hauled around town with great pomp and floral celebration—exactly as South Indian temples do with their own idols. In her book, in fact, Bayly mentions that, for many years, the painted, processional banners were a set of twenty-one flags 'adorned with a striking mixture of Saivite and Vaishnavite sacred symbols', such as a bull representing Shiva's companion Nandi, an eagle representing Vishnu's steed Garuda, and a boar representing Vishnu's Varaha avatar.

The shed was bolted and locked, so Fernando invited me to put my eye up against the wide hinge of a small door, to peer into its soft black interior. 'What do you see?' he asked.

Not a carriage, I told him, but a big golden palanquin, some of its paint peeling, its throne empty.

Fernando said: 'I think that must be the bigger palanquin. It is taken out during the years the Ther isn't. Then there should be a smaller palanquin behind that. Do you see it?' I did. 'That is taken out on the first Saturday of every month. And the Pon Ther is in the next room.'

I stepped back and looked once more at the shed. Something puzzled me, and it took me a couple of minutes before I figured it out: It had no Ther-sized door at all. In front of where the Ther stood, patiently waiting to stretch its legs once every half-decade, there was merely a wall of solid-looking brick.

'That's right,' Fernando said, smiling. 'When it is time for the Ther to be taken out, they demolish the wall. Then they also demolish the section of the compound wall that separates it from the road.' He pointed, and now I saw that half of the compound wall was clearly of a more recent vintage than its other half. 'And then, once the procession is over, they brick the walls up all over again.' With such joyous exertions is the Ther loosed upon Tuticorin every five years.

The Ther's twenty-one processional flags are kept in the custody of the Pandiyapathi, the gentleman whose identity Fernando had promised to explain during my first day in Tuticorin. There were, he said, originally seven Parava villages in the area: Vaiparu,

Vemparu, Veerapandiyapattinam, Tuticorin, Punnakayal, Manapadu and Alanthalai. Each fishing village had its own leader, a hereditary thalaivan. But the chief of chiefs, the foremost amongst the seven leaders was always the thalaivan of Tuticorin, or the jati thalaivan. 'We believe the jati thalaivan's family is descended from one of the Pandya princes,' Fernando said. 'This is why he is known as the Pandiyapathi.'

The current jati thalaivan is J. Berchmans Motha, a militaristic, spare man in his seventies, whom I had spotted in an adjoining pew during Kattar's Mass, sitting without movement for forty-five minutes. Fernando had actually taken me around to his house the previous afternoon, a modest brown bungalow on Kerecope Street, right behind Justin Photo Colour Lab. It was around 2 p.m., and Motha, woken by our incessant ringing of the doorbell in the middle of his siesta, came to the porch tousle-haired and grumpy, admonished Fernando for disturbing him, and asked us to come back another day. It was the only time during my stay in Tuticorin that I saw Fernando at a loss, and it must have lasted all of five minutes.

When we did return, Fernando was careful to call ahead, and we were consequently met by a Motha with neater hair and a lukewarm smile. The smile, gleaned as it has to be through the foliage of his moustache, is not the expression he is most comfortable with. By default, Motha looks deeply disappointed with the human race, much as a father would be with a wastrel son; his eyes, behind spectacles, engage minimally with others, and his conversation is grudgingly given, some mental pair of scales weighing each sentence to judge whether it should be squandered on this undeserving world. But he was never unpleasant, and he was more generous with his time than I could have hoped.

Twenty-two generations ago, Motha's direct ancestor, Joao da Cruz, was the incumbent jati thalaivan who led his people in the conversion to Catholicism. The position has passed from father to son since then, every jati thalaivan serving as a vital liaison between the Paravas on the one hand and the Portuguese and the Church on the other. But the title has never meant as little as it does today. 'It's a sign of the times,' Kattar had told me earlier. 'The people have democratic and economic independence today, so nobody feels the need to look up to Motha, or to accord him the respect they gave their earlier leaders.'

The few customary rights of the jati thalaivan that Motha's father had continued to hold disappeared after 1947, when India became independent. 'My father was a pauper, and he had many enemies,' Motha said. Motha himself joined the merchant navy, starting as a seaman and retiring as a captain. 'There are, perhaps, a few elderly people in Tuticorin who still respect the position of the jati thalaivan,' he said. 'But that is all. Otherwise, I have no friends. I am alone.'

The narrow passageway from Motha's door to his living room is dominated by a large painting on one wall—an oil of a gentleman with a wiggly moustache, whom a floating banner identifies as 'Gabriel Dacrus Vas Gomus Saditaleivar, 1753–1808.' That name would have been prefixed, in correspondence or formal speech, by the Portuguese honorific Senhor Senhor Don. In the painting, Senhor Senhor Don Gabriel Dacrus looks, slightly cross-eyed, at a pearl he holds in one hand, and an emblem of a fish further illustrates his connection to the Parava community. 'This was the ancestor who had the Pon Ther built,' Motha told us. On either side of the painting are mottled black-and-white photographs of Motha's father and grandfather, in long, tapered hats, and of his grandmothers, their earlobes so weighed down by heavy earrings that they had turned into elongated gaskets.

Behind the chair on which I was sitting ('Two hundred years

old, that chair,' I was told) was a dark green, hand-carved section of wood that Motha identified as a portion of an ancestor's palanquin. A pencilled scribble—'1782.22.2'—dated it, he said, 'to around the time the Dutch in these parts were chased out by the British.' Opening the door of the palanquin, he showed us the golden emblem of a regal British lion. 'You see? That was embossed when the jati thalaivan pledged allegiance to Great Britain,' he said. 'But who even knows or wants to know about this kind of thing now?'

Like every old man, Motha bore a generic grudge against the modern world for caring too little for his generation, but his grievances against the Church were far more pointed. The priests who swarmed into Tuticorin after the mass conversion of the 1530s had worked assiduously, he said, to remove every trace of the jati thalaivan's powers. 'Many of them even denied that anything like the hereditary leadership system existed,' he said. 'They'd talk about the chieftains of the individual villages, but they would not acknowledge that there was a supreme leader. But it was only because there was one leader that the whole community could be converted at one go.'

Motha's sentiment formed a part of a curious ambivalence towards the Church that I grew to sense in the Paravas. Their belief in the Catholic faith still runs strong, and a deep

Captain J. Berchmans Motha

knowledge of their Church's history is surprisingly common, as if it had been carried and spread by the region's gigantic flies. When I sat in that staff room in Manapadu, a group of teachers of assorted middle-school subjects debated the chronology and geography of Xavier's travels with the zeal and knowledge of university academics. When I sat in Fernando's mobile recharge shop, he pulled open a drawer and shyly showed me a clutch of notebooks, with page after page of neatly written notes on the history of Tuticorin. I can think of no other mobile recharge shop to offer that sort of service.

But regularly, the Paravas' pride in their past reaches further back, past the advent of the Portuguese, and then it appears laced with regret or anger at the loss of so much heritage. This was true not only of Motha, who had lost something tangible, but of a man like Joe D'Cruz, a Chennai-based author and a successful businessman, and such a human dynamo that it is impossible to sit still next to him. D'Cruz was my gateway into Tuticorin's Parava community; he is so well known there that Fernando lubricated many of my interviews by simply saying: 'Joe sent him.' In our very first conversation, D'Cruz had foreshadowed my meeting with Motha. 'The Church has destroyed the lineage of leadership in Tuticorin. It just used the fishermen to spread Christianity,' he said, as we swung one evening between his house and his office in his car, his BlackBerry emitting occasional, soft chirrups of light. 'My blood is Hindu—it has been for years. Only my name is Christian. Why should I take on an alien culture or religion when my own is so glorious?'

Motha claimed that some of the Church's stated history was sheer fabrication. 'You must have seen the signboard saying that Our Lady of the Snows was consecrated in 1582?' he asked. I nodded. 'Well, it wasn't. The original church was right here, on Kerecope Street, in front of this house,' he said. 'On that site was a lodge for foreign missionaries and travellers. The present church was built only in 1712, but in their history, they have just fused the two buildings.' Motha also insisted that the Church denied the authenticity of one of its relics—a strand of the Virgin Mary's hair—and, in search of proof, stalked away into another room to rummage among some documents. Fernando and I sat very still and looked at each other. Somewhere in the house, a MIDI version of *Silent Night* was playing.

After a few minutes, Motha returned with an armload of files, each sated with thick sheaves of documents. These were letters in English or Tamil or Portuguese, between his ancestors and Portuguese regents or officials of the Church, the papers all jaundiced with age, their edges cracked and curled like untended toenails. Some of these letters Motha had, in the manner of an earnest schoolboy, copied painstakingly onto fresh sheets of ledger paper. 'See here now. This is the certificate of authenticity for that strand of hair, from 1789,' he said, pointing to a letter from a Portuguese Church official. It was nearly falling apart. 'There are even older papers in that room, but they would crumble into a powder with a single touch.'

Even more nefarious motives, according to Motha, were afoot. In the church, he said, his voice dropping a little, there was a box full of the jewels with which the idol of Our Lady of the Snows was decked out for the Pon Ther procession. 'Traditionally, there have been two keys for that box, one kept with the jati thalaivan and one kept with the parish priest,' Motha said. 'But now they're even trying to take that key away from me.' His face clouded with anger. 'The jati thalaivan could hold his own against the Church even until the nineteenth century. But after that, it all just slipped away.'

Motha, a widower, has two daughters, one living in Chennai and one right down the street from him. His only son is a geologist in Australia, and Motha said he was unlikely to return to Tuticorin. If that proves to be the case, Motha will be the last of a grand, centuries-long line of local leaders, rubbed out partly by design but partly also by the inexorable forward march of history. When I understood that, I could understand better his sadness of seeing a noble family tradition wither away on his watch, and his frustration of being able to do nothing about it.

Puzzlingly, throughout the Portuguese presence on this stretch of Tamil Nadu, its cuisine remained as untouched as its religion stood transformed. I came across no Portuguese influences in my meals in Tuticorin and its neighbouring villages, but, thinking I'd missed something or simply eaten in all the wrong places, I later sought the wisdom of Jacob Aruni, a food consultant and researcher in Chennai. 'It's true, and it's a mystery,' Aruni said. 'In Goa, for instance, the use of cinnamon and garlic and wine in food caught on from the Portuguese. But in the coastal area around Tuticorin, they still use salt, tamarind and coconut more dominantly—the ingredients they were using even before the Portuguese arrived.'

Aruni is a queer fish. After graduating with a Bachelor's in Physics, he leaped sideways into the wholly unrelated craft of cooking. He was a chef in the industry for exactly one year when he realized that he would rather be teaching; he was a teacher at a catering college for exactly six years when he realized that he would rather be researching. 'My students would bring their lunch boxes, and I'd always be interested in eating that food, in finding out how it was made, and what people still made at home,' he said. 'So I started researching the cuisines of Tamil Nadu.' Travelling from village to village and invading kitchens with his boundless curiosity, Aruni first dredged out forgotten recipes of the Kongunad region, around Coimbatore, and of Nanjil Nadu, running from Madurai to Kanyakumari. Then, in a streak of culinary archaeology, he resurrected some ancient dishes from the Sangam Era, dug up a strain of cooking that used flowers as primary ingredients, and polished his knowledge of Ayurveda-balanced food.

It was during a trip to Muttom, in the Kanyakumari district, that Aruni first came across a version of 'fish *podi*,' a dried fish powder that he would later find, in other age-old variations, in Nagapattinam, in Velankani and near Tuticorin—'in fact, in every single fisherman's house I ever visited in Tamil Nadu.' The *podi*, Aruni insisted, was a singularly Tamil preparation. 'It isn't there in Andhra Pradesh or Kerala or anywhere else. It's ideal for fishing families, really. It doesn't spoil, because it has been dried, and it can use whatever fish they have left over, even tiny prawns that they'd never be able to sell. With it, you just need hot, steamed rice, and you have a meal.'

Aruni described the oldest, most basic version of the *podi* for me. First the fish—any fish—was cubed and fried. Then grated coconut, peppercorns, cumin, curry leaves and raw rice were individually roasted and dried out in the sun. In the final step, the fried fish and the roasted ingredients were combined and pulverised. 'Some versions use coriander seeds, and others use fried tamarind,' Aruni said. 'The powder keeps for ages. I always have three large jars of these powders on hand at home.'

A couple of days later, Aruni scooped out a hefty portion of his dried mackerel *podi* and sent it to me in a plastic tub. The *podi* looked like powdery jaggery, speckled white in places with coconut, and it had a deep, spicy aroma, shot through with the strong presence of fish. Tasted raw, it races to the back of your throat and proceeds to set your tonsils on fire, but with rice and a liberal spoon of ghee, it settles down and thereafter only singes your mouth with occasional bursts of playful fieriness. But Aruni had selected his mackerel well: They were mackerel with character, bursting out of their envelope of spice like strong actors out of a crowded script. For at least two days, the room where I opened Aruni's tub smelled faintly and deliciously of spiced, fried fish. If this was what the good fishermen of Manapadu offered Francis Xavier in his seaside grotto—and they very well may have—I can understand why he decided to stay.

One day, I accompanied Father Kattar to Veerapandiyapattinam, his home village of roughly five thousand fishermen, forty-five minutes' drive from Tuticorin and less than two kilometres from the temple town of Tiruchendur. It was the feast day of St. Thomas, Veerapandiyapattinam's patron saint, and Kattar had been invited to participate in the evening's Mass. 'You know, Xavier once wrote to Rome that the residents of Veerapandiyapattinam were practitioners of sorcery,' Kattar said with a smile. Nearly everybody in the village is a Catholic now, and the focus of the town is the Gothic-styled Church of St. Thomas, dating back to 1886. The church is a long building with a bright white, vaulted ceiling and an inexplicable, cement-coloured finish, as if it were forever young, forever on the verge of being completed.

In the hour before Mass began, Kattar went to visit his mother, and Fernando took me to Father Stephen Gomez, a loose-limbed, thoughtful, middle-aged priest who is the director of the Valampurinatham Institute for Research in Society and Religion, located barely a kilometre from the Church of St. Thomas. Gomez listened politely to Fernando's introduction (which included the statutory mention of Joe D'Cruz) and to my expressed interest in the religious history of the Parava community. 'Yes, it's an interesting subject,' he said finally. Gomez was the only person to articulate what I'd found so fascinating about the Paravas: 'The community has, in a way, fossilised in the state that it was four hundred years ago.' He waved an arm vaguely to his right. 'That church is the centre of their daily lives,' he said. 'Their houses are built around it, and their lives revolve around it.'

The glowing twilight slowly dwindled into a pensive dusk, and the front steps of the Church of St. Thomas came alive with harsh tube lights and the hubbub of its parishioners' conversation. I stood for a while just outside the church, with a group of men that had arrived too late for seats within. Later, I went up to the balcony where, in front of a circular mural of Christ and his disciples, I watched the choir, led by a short organist with jasmine flowers in her hair, her electronic keyboard rattling off many of the same disco classics I heard at Our Lady of the Snows. Looking down from that balcony, I could see the entire length of the church, the multicoloured saris and shirts of the congregation looking like the individual panels of a very big work of stained glass.

The service was first led by a woman, and half an hour into the proceedings, when she issued an instruction, many of the men in her audience stood up and slipped on shoulder vestments, either in red or blue. (They also had circular headbands, which to a man they delayed putting on until the last possible minute, keeping them tucked under their arms.) 'These are the two sabhas,' Fernando told me. Then, searching for the right English word, he said: 'They are the groups of acolytes.' And this proved to be the case: At some point, they took up a cross and banners and candles and moved in a procession into the verandah of the church, where we were already standing. Near us, an orchestra of pipes and drums burst into song.

The ceremony on the verandah was brief and completely unintelligible. Kattar, Gomez and a third priest took their seats, and for fifteen minutes, various speeches were delivered into microphones, only to rebound immediately from the massive speakers placed around us, the words rushing to fuse with their predecessors like mad little droplets of mercury. It didn't seem to disturb my peers in the audience, who listened with rapt attention. 'You should really be here tomorrow,' my neighbour informed me. 'All the children in the village attend, dressed in white and holding candles. It's a beautiful scene.'

After the ceremony, it remained only for Kattar to deliver his Tamil sermon, which he did with his trademark, swerving style. He lectured on truth, seemingly extempore, for several minutes, leaping athletically from quote to quote; in one three-minute sequence alone, I recognized verbatim references from Mahatma Gandhi, Sarvepalli Radhakrishnan and the *Brihadaranyaka Upanishad*, and there were probably more that I missed. When I met him immediately afterwards, at a hurried dinner for a small jumble of priests and invitees, I found that Kattar had barely broken a sweat, his galloping oratory and the close atmosphere of the church notwithstanding. 'It went well, I thought,' he said.

On our drive back to Tuticorin, Kattar was in an expansive mood. 'This is what I missed in Rome, the ability to interact with the people,' he said. 'In all my previous rotations in villages here, I would know every single person. I'd be called upon to mediate disputes. I'd be invited to their homes. I'd be asked to bless the newborn children of even Hindu families. I'd feel involved, and the people would respond with their warmth and love.' We drove on, the shrubby land around us painted in darkness and the road vanishing a few feet from our headlights. Somewhere, off to our right, I could hear a melancholy wind sighing over the slumbering sea.

4
On an odyssey through toddy shops

If you ever find yourself on one of Kerala's highways with an hour or five to spare, keep your eyes open for a distinctive black-and-white signboard by the side of the road. This board will have, in its centre, the single word 'Kallu' in Malayalam, and above it, a legend like 'T. S. No. 189,' the number being subject to change. If a few kilometres go by and you spot no such board—which in itself would be remarkable—you should flag down the first passing male cyclist or pedestrian and say just one word with a questioning drawl: 'Shaaaaaap?' If it is particularly early in the morning, throw in a sheepish smile for good measure.

You must note here that the drawl is everything. If you simply say 'shop,' you will get either an indifferent shrug or a vague gesture towards an establishment selling soap, toothbrushes and packets of potato chips. If, however, you get it right and say 'Shaaaaaap?—like 'sharp' but without the burr—you will get an animated nod and detailed directions to the nearest toddy shop.

More often than not, you will then drive up to a walled-off compound that has one little structure easily identified as the kitchen, another little structure with bicycles parked outside it, and a number of individual little cabanas. There is, unfortunately, an explicit social code that kicks in at the shop's gate. If you happen to look like a local or a paddy field worker, you will be led towards the common bar area; if you don't, you will be requested, equally firmly, to take any of the cabanas that are free. Mixing is discouraged. If you insist on the common bar for yourself, you will get nothing more than a dirty look, but it will be a very dirty look indeed.

The more upscale cabanas, you will find, are furnished with a small ceiling fan, thinly padded benches around a table, an asbestos roof, and chicken wire windows. Curtains are optional. The toddy will be brought to you either in a pitcher or in tall Kingfisher beer bottles, with glasses or earthen tumblers on the side. And then, inevitably, you will ask for something to eat with your toddy, and thus wander into a whole new subculture of food.

The best toddy, toddy that is fresh and untouched by base additives, should taste only marginally less mild than milk, with a slight sweetness, a faint note of ferment, and the occasional granule of coconut husk. When it is collected as sap from the palm tree, the toddy is entirely non-alcoholic, and it is thrown into ferment only when it picks up tiny residues of yeast from the air. Tapped early in the day or late the previous night, it would have barely begun to turn into alcohol, so stories of how, in the olden days, the rich owners of coconut groves would knock back five or six glasses every morning for their health seem entirely plausible. As much as it sounds like an invitation into dipsomania, the best toddy at a toddy shop is to be had at around eleven in the morning.

By lunchtime, the toddy's sweetness will begin to fade, and a few hours after that, questionable practices slip into operation like well-worked gears. A shaaaaaap owner will dump sugar into his toddy to make it more palatable. He will ramp up the kick of the drink, pouring in cheap vodka or dubious arrack or country liquor. Some owners, I was told, powder dried marijuana leaves, tie them into a bundle of thin cotton cloth, and soak the bundles in the toddy. Mahesh Thampy, a friend living in Trivandrum, has heard even more horrific stories, of old batteries dropped into vats of toddy, for the acid to mix slowly with the alcohol.

'You have to remember, most of the people who go to these shops just want to get high as fast as possible and leave,' said Thampy. 'Nobody wants to sit around and drink the good stuff. Which is why there is so much bad liquor floating around, so many newspaper headlines of blindness or even death because of illicit alcohol.' He told me one fantastic story of sitting in a bar in Trivandrum. 'Suddenly there was a power cut, and the lights went out. In the silence, one agonized voice cried out: "Oh my god! I've gone blind!"'

The arrack-mixed toddy, in local parlance, is called '*aana mayaki*,' which reassures its drinkers that it is strong enough to addle an elephant. 'It's all controlled by the liquor mafia here in Kerala, of course,' Thampy said. 'Two or three years ago, somebody calculated that even if every coconut tree in Kerala was tapped, you wouldn't get the volume of toddy that is being served in the state.' Trivandrum has its share of liquor plenipotentiaries, including one gentleman who goes by the zippy label of Yamaha Surendran. Thampy promised he wasn't making that name up.

Meeting Thampy was my introduction to a world where, I was told, work stops for toddy. Thampy is a clean-cut, neatly moustached man who runs a thriving real-estate business in Trivandrum. He has an MBA, and he is intelligent and earnest about his work. But on a Monday morning, he was still eager to troop out of town, onto the highway, in search of a good toddy shop. Indeed, the only person who showed any alarm at all at our agenda was our peach-fuzzed young cabbie, smiling nervously as he examined the prospects of an afternoon of driving drunks around the countryside.

We began inauspiciously. When we entered our first toddy shop, the owner personally came out to discourage us with vigorous gestures from staying, claiming that he had no good toddy on hand. For a barkeep to turn away paying customers seemed astounding, but it confirmed what Thampy had told me about the rigid product differentiation—about how certain types of toddy are only sold to certain types of people. I had exactly five minutes to mull over that nugget of economics in the cab before we stopped again, at a 'toddy garden' further down the same road.

In one of the seven cabanas with wine-red curtains and blue wooden benches, we were brought our toddy, as pale white as diluted buttermilk, served in earthen pots. On the tongue, the toddy fizzed gently, a mild and lazy alcohol that sauntered down your throat. Thampy sipped twice and proclaimed it fresh and 'very decent' compared to some of the toddy he'd had before. I wasn't going to point out that, in comparison to battery-acid toddy, that was no great accreditation.

Toddy-shop food is strategically kicked into a high orbit of spice, so that customers constantly demand more toddy to soothe their flaming tongues. Our mussels, which arrived first, had been quick-roasted with coconut, curry leaves and coriander, and then buried under lashings of chilli powder. Done differently, in another dish, the mussels looked like giant spiders that had waded heroically through batter only to then accidentally fall into hot coconut oil.

But the staple of every toddy shop is its kappa-meen curry

combination. The kappa—bland, steamed lumps of tapioca, tempered with coconut and chillies—is such dense starch that, according to the laws of physics, light should not be able to escape it. It would be inedible without its thin, oil-slicked fish curry that, in happy symbiosis, would in turn be inedible without the kappa. All toddy shop meen curries come furiously red with industrial dosages of chilli powder. In the average curry, the fish is incidental, a temporary tenant in, rather than the owner of, its overwhelming gravy. The question of which fish you would like in your curry is perfunctory and academic; you won't be able to tell the difference.

At the toddy garden, Thampy also ordered a karimeen, a perfectly shaped pearl spot fish that was hollowed out, stuffed with masala, fried to a fantastic crisp, and served whole. 'But this,' he intoned, after two bites, 'This is a fake.' Made in China, did he mean? In a sweatshop, to a template exported from Kerala? 'It isn't karimeen. It's some other fish that they're passing off as pearl spot, and charging pearl spot prices for it.' The dastardliness of it all seemed to move him deeply, and he buttonholed our waiter to ask where our fish was from. 'The river fish is from Quilon,' the waiter offered. 'And the sea fish—that's from just down the road.'

By 'just down the road' he meant Vizhinjam, a port of ancient, ancient vintage, and one of the deepest natural harbours in India. In a smooth crescent of water and shore, watched over by an incongruously new beige-and-white mosque and a church of Portuguese construction from the 1500s, was a swarm of anchored fishing boats. On the quay, outboard motors, pulled out and oiled, were racked methodically like black metal carcasses. Intriguing clusters of cleaned, empty cans of Servo engine oil sat near the waterfront. An auto-rickshaw puttered around, wheezing, while a loudspeaker mounted on its top shouted out the dates of a speaking tour of a roster of Christian priests.

It was quite by accident that we ran into Mariadasan and heard his story. In plastic red-and-black slippers, a blue shirt, and a flawless white mundu edged in gold, he was standing at the edge of the quay, looking out to sea and gorging himself on the delicious, salt-flecked breeze. He must have seen us poking curiously at one of the giant clumps of palm and coconut fronds on the quay, because he walked over to us, stood there patiently until we had poked to our satisfaction, and then said: 'It's for the GPS.'

We pretended to understand, but only for a few seconds. So he explained: 'When we go out to sea, we plant these in the ocean, and we track their coordinates on the GPS.' In these bobbing tangles of vegetation, the fish would lay their eggs and begin to lead a comfortable middle-class existence—until, a few months later, the fishermen would return, guided unerringly by their GPS, to simply scoop these residents of suburbia into their holds.

Every single boat in this harbour had a GPS system in its cabin, Mariadasan said, and he invited us onto his craft, the *Julymol*, to take a look. Swaggering a little now, enjoying the interest, Mariadasan hitched up his mundu and began to show us around his compact boat—the yawning mouth of the hold; the giant wad of orange nylon net, as thick and wide as a queen-sized mattress; long bamboo poles with Servo cans tied to them as flotation devices. 'We plant those poles in the water where we have our underwater nets,' Mariadasan said. 'In the daytime, there's a flag at the top, and at night, a flashlight. That way, other approaching boats know exactly where they shouldn't go.'

Inside the cramped cabin, Mariadasan pointed lovingly to his GPS, and then in succession to an echo sounder, a wireless, and a CD player. 'Look, listen,' he said, and switched the player on. From tinny speakers poured an approximation of 1980s British pop, garbled but insistent. When Mariadasan wasn't looking, I pressed the Eject button on the CD player, eager to find out who the band was. Out popped the CD, pasted over with a label of a naked woman, hands demurely covering her nipples. Very efficient, I thought to myself—two forms of entertainment in one.

The *Julymol* sails with a crew of between eight and ten, Mariadasan told us. 'We sail for about twenty-four hours, to find our spot. Then we drop anchor and fish.' The boat remains at sea for as many as twenty days at a time, by which time, Mariadasan admitted, the first day's catch begins to smell somewhat rank. Then they set off for home, with fish worth about Rs 4 lakh in their holds.

On one trip in 2004, Mariadasan, who lived in Mumbai at the time, strayed into Pakistani waters. At the time, he was thirty-five, and he had two sons in school. 'I didn't even know if I'd ever see them again.' Mariadasan and eight other fishermen were imprisoned in a Karachi jail, and fed almost exclusively on five rotis and three cups of tea a day. 'We were beaten a little when we were first caught, but luckily, we'd just managed to radio out for help before they picked us up,' he said. Ten months later, with some new wounds and scars, all nine were released. Mariadasan packed up and returned to Kerala—just in time for the Indian Ocean tsunami to hit the state's coast that December.

That year, travelling down the coast of Tamil Nadu in the aftermath of the tsunami, I had seen something of its pitiless impact on fishing villages and harbours. 'Was there much destruction here?' I asked, already prepared to commiserate and condole with him and his inevitably woeful story. 'Did many fishermen die?'

'Oh no,' Mariadasan replied. 'It was the day after Christmas.

Nobody here was at sea. We were all still sleeping off the previous day's toddy hangover.'

In Kerala, where toddy is as much of a state passion as football or Communism, canvassing views about the relative merits of various toddies is a thankless venture. Every man will have an opinion, for starters, and he will not be stopped until he has expounded every facet of it, accompanied wherever possible by proof of a practical nature. The only vote that approaches anything resembling unanimity is about where in Kerala the best toddy is to be found. That would be in the Alappuzha district, which has long operated under the alias of Alleppey, drawing tourists to its backwaters as a siren would Ithacans. Alleppey is the toddy shop mother lode, where shops glint like nuggets every few metres.

The town of Alleppey is only a few hours away from Trivandrum by train, but that brief trip may as well have taken us into a different quadrant of the world altogether. Trivandrum was dusty and, even at 5 a.m. on a February morning, sticky and airless. Alleppey, at half past eight the same day, was fresh and cool, newly washed by rain, its waters and trees gleaming silver and gold. It was a perfect time to be outdoors. Purely in the interests of research, though, we were in a toddy shop cabana an hour later, by about 10 a.m.

There is a word to be said here about rooting out the best toddy shop in an unfamiliar town. We stumbled onto the most ideal method by chance—to commandeer an auto-rickshaw and solicit its driver's guidance. The auto-rickshaw driver will be immediately so struck by appearance of people after his own heart—people, in other words, who will get out of an early morning train, exit the station, and ask for a toddy shop—that he may even forget to inflate his rate.

Our man steered us unhesitatingly to T. S. No. 86, calling it
one of the most highly recommended toddy shops in Alleppey—
thirty years old, plying four hundred customers with toddy every
day. It sits off a narrow stretch of a highway, opposite paddy
fields with water lilies growing out of their banks of water. Its
nerve centre is a two-room affair of kitchen and pantry, and it
has four or five cabanas in its yard. It would be too much to say
you can't miss it—you can very easily miss it, in fact. But you
shouldn't.

This shop's prep kitchen consisted of a couple of tree stumps
out back, near a small stream. Having ordered what I hoped was
un-faux karimeen, I was shown the gills of the fish, still red,
proof that it was fresh. Then our sous-chef peeled the fish like a
potato, hacking off the scales with a knife, revealing flesh the
colour of pale twilight. For the tougher scales on the top and the
back of the fish, he used scissors. From a slit, he felt around
with a couple of fingers and pulled out the innards, like a
magician extracting streamers from his sleeve. The karimeen then
moved into the kitchen, where on a ledge of stone, a wok full of
coconut oil was already sitting on a stove. Next to it was a
colander, bearing what I was told were turtle parts. On an open
wood fire in another corner, a heavy pot of rice muttered quietly
away to itself.

In this kitchen, I finally had a chance to see exactly how much
spice went into toddy shop food. The most reliable measure
seemed to simply be: A lot. In a little stainless steel bowl, our
chef mixed red chilli powder, black pepper, garam masala, salt,
turmeric and water, making a paste that was a dark, brooding
vermilion. Into this went the karimeen, the paste worked into its
slits with a finger; it marinated there for a while, and then slipped
into its jacuzzi of coconut oil.

Coconut oil is a funny thing. Outside Kerala, it is known,
thanks to the Parachute brand, as primarily a hair-care product,

to be taken off the bathroom shelf on Sundays for a ritual oil bath. In Kerala, it is the frying medium of choice. The mind, of course, knows this vital difference, but as I discovered, the nose does not. When that karimeen hit its wok of oil, there was an overwhelming burst of smell, like an explosion in the Parachute factory. And somehow it smelled very familiar and yet very wrong, as if somebody had decided to make tea with Head & Shoulders or salad dressing out of Brylcreem.

Eyes streaming, I escaped the kitchen into the pantry next door, where, as fortune would have it, the toddy was just being brought in. In most shops, the toddy is stored in huge, black plastic cans that look suspiciously like former containers for kerosene. Here, the toddy was strained through three separate filters, to catch bits of husk and other impurities, caught in white plastic jugs and then decanted into old Kingfisher beer bottles. This toddy had been tapped just a couple of hours earlier, still so sweet that, when it was brought to our table, it managed to attract fruit flies out of nowhere. It was thicker and fizzier than at Trivandrum, backed by the unmistakable aftertaste of fresh coconut, and with only a sotto whisper of alcohol.

The karimeen arrived soon after, brown as toast, wrapped inside its greatcoat of masala, and dressed with black pepper and raw onions. It was a bony fish, but its meat was soft, picked apart by fingers almost as easily as cotton candy. This was magnificent eating—crisped masala, cut by the sweetness of the fish and the tartness of a squeeze of lemon. Mahesh Thampy, it turned out, was right. If this was real karimeen, the fish at the toddy shop in Trivandrum was a certain imposter.

The fish curry, on the other hand, was beginning to increasingly seem to me like an acquired taste. As at Trivandrum, it arrived in seething red attire, and more mystifyingly, it arrived cold—yesterday's curry, with hunks of fresh-fried kaari fish slipped in. The kaari was dense and chewy, its flesh looking like boiled potato. I closed my eyes, dunked a piece of kappa into the curry, and concentrated on really tasting it—and I could still taste nothing but the aggressive rawness of the chilli powder.

When I opened my eyes, my Malayali friend across the table had his eyes shut as well. Then he opened them, looked at me, and said: 'That was heaven. That tasted like my childhood.'

Our auto-rickshaw driver insisted that we try one more toddy shop nearby, where we stayed away from the toddy and just asked for any fish that was fresh from the backwaters. We got, first, a plate of fried chembelli, a small, inexpensive fish that tasted chewy and fibrous, like a better class of cardboard. Then we got a hideous looking fish called the beral. Deprived of its fins, the beral's long, thick body looked almost snakelike, and its face was thuggish—definitely the sort of fish to avoid meeting in a dark, deserted bend of the river. But I had maligned the beral too soon. Its homely features concealed, if not a heart of gold, at least fresh, smooth meat and a crisp skin.

By lunchtime, we were in the poignant situation of already having eaten the equivalent of three lunches. It had grown suddenly warm, my friend's head began to loll in sleep, and I was shuddering at the thought of meeting another masala-heavy product of the backwaters. All three issues were simultaneously addressed by that

A toddy shop, off a highway near Alleppey

marvellous mode of transport: The Backwaters Bus. The Backwaters Bus seems to have been created, in some part, as an exercise in voyeurism. With around eighty passengers on board, at Rs 10 a head, it ambles from Alleppey to Kottayam in four hours, through a maze of vegetation-clogged creeks that appear impossible to remember or navigate. But the only time it really slows down from its amble to a shuffle is in relatively open waters, apparently to give every passenger a view of the bizarre houseboats all around.

The most basic houseboats were the most logically constructed ones—long, with a single cabin, and extensive deck space. One level up, the slightly larger houseboats warranted a raised sun deck of sorts, where a couple of lounge chairs could sit on either side of a table of drinks. So far, so good.

But then, in a single, befuddling leap, came the top-of-the-line houseboats—raised sun deck, extensive hardwood furniture, baroque cabinets, satellite dishes, and plasma TV sets. It was in one of these that I saw a group of four people, sitting with their backs to the water, watching a golf game on television. Behind me, from the commuters on my Backwaters Bus, there were titters at that surreal vision, and nudges to neighbours to look-look-look. In one stroke, the sightseers had become the sightseen.

It would have been only too easy, I thought, for the residents of this gorgeous district to resent intruders, to be reluctant to share their gold-dappled green waters with anybody else, much less with eyesore houseboats and plasma TVs. But I sensed that nowhere in Alleppey, and it wasn't just the dry logic of capitalism, of how tourism had improved everybody's standard of living. Instead, it tended more towards the sort of benevolent tolerance with which grandparents regard grandchildren with wayward minds. As the Backwaters Bus cleared the open waters and entered a tributary on the other side, a few people exchanged amused smiles, shook their heads in mock wonder, and returned to their newspapers for the rest of the ride.

⌒

Later that evening, at Kottayam, our palates rebelled furiously, wanting something other than fish fried in coconut oil. It was a notable meal, if only to observe, in the interests of science, what we ordered instead. My friend, the Malayali, ordered beef fried in coconut oil. And I? I ordered curd and rice—soothing white, free of belligerent masala and pools of silvery grease and shards of bone and the arresting taste of fish. It was heaven. It tasted like my childhood.

⌒

The quintessential toddy shop in Kerala is still a male bastion—unsurprisingly, in a state that its residents say is still a deeply conservative one. 'Just yesterday afternoon,' Mahesh Thampy had told me, 'I saw three local women standing at a pushcart, eating a few dosas off paper plates. And people stared incessantly, very unused to even that simple sight.'

But in the last few years, two elevating things have happened. The toddy shop, long a part of authentic Kerala, has now become a part of Authentic Kerala, the tourist-brochure version of the state, and female visitors will not be denied their right to sit in cabanas and order toddy and karimeen. Also, the subculture of toddy shop food has begun to be celebrated, and the food desired not merely as incendiary accompaniment to liquor but in its own right. Enter, then, the toddy parlour. Even its nomenclature is such a far cry from that of the toddy shop that it deserves commentary. The toddy 'shop' indicates the most basic of transactions, where money changes hands, a product is sold, and the customer heads for the exit. With toddy, the process is only slightly less rapid. Few of the paddy field workers, itinerant cyclists or other local drinkers wish to actually tarry in a toddy shop longer than it takes to knock back a few glasses, so that the alcohol can hot up the blood faster and cheaper. The toddy 'parlour,' on the other hand, carries the weight of both etymology and custom. The word 'parlour' comes from the French 'parler,' to talk, and a room thus dubbed becomes an open invitation to shoot the breeze. But the genteelness and almost Victorian delicacy we have come to associate with a parlour sits amiss with the grime and the focussed alcoholism of the toddy shop.

The two most famous specimens of these toddy parlours, known as far away as Cochin and Trivandrum, sit on the road from Kottayam to Pallom, barely a kilometre from each other, and are bitter rivals in court to boot. The original, Kariumpumkala, started life as a genuine toddy shop in 1958, and although it became known for its superior food, it held on to those roots. But in 2001, when the Kerala government suspended all toddy shop licenses in a brave, and vain, attempt to discourage drinking, Kariumpumkala won through that awful year solely on the strength of its food. When the licenses were restored, one year later, Kariumpumkala didn't even try to apply for one; it had found its new direction.

Kariumpumkala today is a slightly ghastly brick-and-mortar structure, painted in shades of green and pink. Its top two storeys are air-conditioned, every floor is tiled, and the tabletops are made of granite. Over the billing counter is a shelf full of trophies that Kariumpumkala has won in something called the Philips Food Fest. But most heartbreaking of all is a perverse remembrance of times past—a sign that says 'Smoking, alcohols strictly prohibited'.

Kariumpumkala's present owner would talk of none of this. He was obsessed, instead, with his legal battle with Karimpinkala, the upstart establishment down the road that, he claimed, had stolen and only slightly modified his restaurant's name. 'That isn't the real one,' he said repeatedly. But Karimpinkala still serves toddy, and Kariumpumkala does not. That little edge makes all the difference in the sweeps to win Kerala's hearts and minds.

In the leafy parking lot of Karimpinkala, a 'Toddy Shop And A/c Family Restaurant', we found Maruti Swift cars and gleaming SUVs, and cabanas that were closer in size to mid-level dorm rooms. We sat under fans, on plastic chairs that skidded on the tiled floors, and drummed our fingers on a glass-topped table. We were handed a menu, laminated in clear plastic. Apart from the 'Sweet and cold coconut toddy', we could have ordered Diet Coke, Fanta, the enigmatic 'Soda B & S', or ice cream. We could even have asked for that most pan-Indian of dishes, Gobi Manchurian. As we sat staring a little disbelievingly at that menu, another SUV pulled up outside. A family dismounted—parents, little children, and even a grandmother—and stormed into one of the other cabanas. We were, most definitely, not in Kansas any more.

Karimpinkala's toddy, served in small earthen jugs, was thick, faintly stale, and tasted of sediment. But its star turn came in the form of its karimeen polichchathu—fish that was steamed in its marinade rather than fried, wrapped in a banana leaf, and served under a canopy of curry leaves, onions and red pepper flakes. And so I finally managed to grasp the flavour of the pearl spot itself—a tart, citrusy tang, but warmed with the heat of spice, as delicious as a mildly sunny sky.

Jijin, our auto-rickshaw driver for the day, had by now cottoned on to our routine, and when we left Karimpinkala, he said: 'But you should also try *mundhiri kallu*'—literally, raisin toddy—'because that's a specialty here.' Between the months of November and March, Jijin explained, toddy-shop owners slipped raisins into the evening toddy and served it the next morning, when the raisins had drunk their fill and fattened into triple their size. 'Although these days,' he said, as he started to scour the sides of the road leading to Kumarakom, 'people get cheap and just add grape juice to give it the same flavour.'

We found no *mundhiri kallu* at our first stop, a whitewashed toddy shop set back so far from the road on its dusty little plot that it looked like a Last Chance Saloon in the American West. By this time, it was noon, and hot outdoors, but the shop was dark and cool inside. The day's toddy had lost some of its sweetness by then, and it was bubbling energetically as it fermented. We still managed a few glasses each, Jijin included— which may well have explained his subsequent, intemperate willingness to let us have a go at driving his auto-rickshaw in turns to the next toddy shop.

In our cool, dark shack-cabana, we ordered a couple of bottles of *mundhiri kallu*, which turned out to be a pale pink concoction, reminiscent of Pepto-Bismol. At the bottom of the bottles were thick layers of white sediment, and the swollen corpses of raisins bobbed in the toddy. It tasted, to my mind, just the same as regular toddy, although the raisins served as occasional happy surprises, bursting with a concentrated blast of sweetness.

'In the villages, the sediment is very important,' Jijin said. 'They add water to it and then mix it into the batter for appams, to make the appams soft.'

'I see,' I said.

'So people come to the toddy shops and take this sediment away. In the cities, of course, they just buy yeast.' Jijin paused here and mulled. 'Yeast works too.'

There was a further comfortable silence. Then Jijin, expounding further on the sediment, said: 'They make a type of vinegar from it as well.'

'How?' I asked.

It was the wrong question to pose. Jijin lapsed into deep

thought, emerging only after many minutes to drink more *mundhiri kallu*. I drank more *mundhiri kallu* as well. At some later point, the three of us may or may not have sworn to each other to never forget this moment, and that we were all brothers, man, whatever our differences, we were all brothers, well, in a manner of speaking, and that it was important not to lose this— *this*, you know, this connection—never lose that, man. And then we tripped our way back towards the auto-rickshaw, and Jijin drove us to Kumarakom and bundled us onto the bus to Kochi.

Accepted wisdom has it that only in the south of Kerala is the food so fiery, because of its insistence on wading into the chilli and kokum. In the north, curries are tempered with more coconut or coconut milk, taking the sharp edges off the spices. I was curious to see how that principle worked in toddy shops in the north, around Kochi or Kozhikode, but first we had to find some. If Alleppey was the mother lode and the area around Trivandrum was a vein of dubious quality, north Kerala resembled an abandoned shaft, mined clean of all ore. In Kochi, we found one toddy shop purely by accident—in the Jewish Quarter near Fort Cochin, an open-fronted establishment that was very obviously a tourist hook but that nonetheless served some good toddy. Driving out of Kozhikode, we had to look for forty minutes before we found a toddy shop. In that time, in Alleppey, we would have found ten.

The mechanics of toddy shop commerce, we discovered in Kozhikode, changed for no man, not even for a north Keralite. The karimeen curry—or as it was known in these parts, the erimeen curry—still came to the table as bellicose a red as in the south, still singeing the back of the mouth on its way down. The chembelli was still fried in the same masala, and it still tasted of cardboard. The coconut-heavy cooking of the outside world had been stopped and turned away on the threshold of the toddy shop kitchen. The food still left you gasping and sweating, the glasses of water—tinted pink, as always, by a purifying tree bark called Pathimukam—were still laughably inadequate, and I still found myself hollering hoarsely for toddy, for its milky sweetness to put the fire out.

My original rationalization for the sparser occurrence of toddy shops in this region had been the most obvious one: This was an area with a much higher concentration of Muslims than the south, and so consequently a higher concentration of firm teetotallers. But our guide, Madhu Madhavan, a young Kochi-based radio producer of great spirit and enterprise, was not so sure of our theory, so he undertook to interrogate the toddy shop proprietor about it.

'Nonsense,' our host said brusquely. 'The Muslims drink just as much as the rest of us. More, probably.'

As our theory melted into puddles around our feet, the proprietor must have seen our stricken faces, looking like the last flat-earthers hearing about Magellan's voyage of circumnavigation. More gently, he said: 'Well, maybe they do it at home rather than out in public. But they all certainly drink, there's no doubt about that.'

He transacted some business at his till, saw that we were still standing there, and said, by way of coded closure: 'There are more toddy shops in the areas where the communists are in power.'

This made little sense to me, but standing outside the toddy shop, Madhu interpreted it for us. 'He's talking about the biggest caste in Kerala, the Iravas, who have traditionally been toddy tappers,' he said. One of the proposed origins of the very word 'Irava' is the old Tamil word for toddy, 'iizham,' and some legend has it that the Iravas even brought the coconut palm from Sri Lanka to India.

In north Kerala, the Iravas have come to be known as the Thiyyas. 'The Thiyyas occupy a slightly higher position in the caste hierarchy, and they think that toddy tapping as a profession is beneath them,' Madhu said. There is, therefore, less tapping in the north; much of the toddy that is served near Kochi and Kozhikode is transported there from the districts of Alleppey or Palakkad. 'And there's a rule of thumb—a huge part of the Communist Party membership is made up of Iravas,' Madhu said. Even a body like the Sree Narayana Dharma Paripalana Yogam, a social reform organization working for the Irava community, steadily started, in the 1950s, to lose its members to the Communist movement, as Thomas Johnson Nossiter points out in his book *Communism in Kerala*. 'So the Iravas tap the toddy, and where the Communists dominate, they get licenses easily and set up their shops,' Madhu said. 'I've heard of officials in Irava organizations in Alleppey who own chains of toddy shops there.'

As Madhu spoke, and even later as I was looking up the histories of the Iravas, of Communism in Kerala, and of toddy shops, my mind's eye kept flicking back to that single whitewashed toddy shop outside Kottayam, that Wild West saloon transplanted out of its own space and time. It had looked so basic and peaceful, without a hint that it existed where it did because of statewide politicking and a centuries-old caste system. The confluence of politics, religion and society can wash over every single particle of life—even something as fundamental as the toddy shop, born out of the simplest of man's desires: to get off the road, out of the sun, and get a drink.

5

On searching for a once-lost love

To attempt to write with enthusiasm about food, I have discovered, requires two great qualities: the ability to eat with a catholic, voluminous appetite, and the ability to eat out alone. The first is a purely physical constraint. A. J. Liebling, the emperor of gourmandizing writers, once pointed out that the average day presented, to the members of his tribe, only two opportunities for really extensive fieldwork: lunch and dinner. 'They are not to be wasted minimizing the intake of cholesterol,' Liebling wrote. 'They are indispensable, like a prizefighter's hours on the road.' (If his monumental waistline was not proof enough that Liebling practised what he preached, his accounts of his meals are; at one lunch, with a friend, he consumed a whole trout with butter, a Provencal meat stew, and a young, roasted guinea hen, with the appropriate wines and a bottle and a half of champagne. Then, presumably, there was dessert.)

But even a weak appetite can be cultivated and expanded, if not to Lieblingian proportions then at least to a point of modest adventurousness. The ability to dine out alone, however, seems to be like the ability to curl your tongue—either you have it or you don't. Those who don't have it tell me that it is just an insuperable mental block. I once heard of a software engineer, on deputation in the United States, who worked late hours and came back to his hotel well after room service had ceased room servicing. The coffee shop downstairs was open all night, but so reluctant was our friend to sit in a restaurant by himself and eat a sandwich that he simply skipped dinner. For the entire month.

Fortunately, I have always been made of tougher material; nothing would induce me to skip dinner. Often, in fact, when I've been travelling, I've actually preferred to eat alone, and not only because it enables a silent, more intimate communion with my food. A restaurant, particularly during a weekday afternoon, is like a finger on the pulse of a town. People come in with distinct agendas, even if the agenda is not to have one. They make business deals, argue over sports and politics, court each other, ignore each other, spend time with family, suffer the company of colleagues, or, like me, sit in a corner by themselves and watch it all over the top of a newspaper. And in the manner of a primitive cultural anthropologist, I lap it up in fascination, convinced that I am seeing the life of the town unfold in front of me. Maybe I am; or maybe I'm just seeing people eat lunch.

The only major disadvantage to eating in solitude, especially in a town that one doesn't know very well, is figuring out where to eat. Asking in your hotel will only earn you a warm recommendation for the hotel's own restaurants. Asking the wrong people—and it's impossible to know who the wrong people are until you've eaten in the places they suggest—will lead you to the sort of food they *think* you want to eat, rather than the food they would themselves eat, which is also the food you really want to eat. On a vacation, of course, the joys of wandering around and of serendipitous discovery are all very well. But it must be most disheartening, for food writers as well as serious gourmands, to come away from a place only to discover that they had been sucked in by a succession of tourist-trap restaurants, all the while ignoring the authentic, wholly brilliant eatery just next door to their hotel.

This was the position I found myself in on my first afternoon in Mangalore. I had taken an overnight train from Cochin, waking just in time to see the pastels of morning wash over the serene beginnings of the Konkan Coast. The half-light conferred a magic upon otherwise ordinary sights. Sitting next to the window, I gawked at everything that passed by me—deserted sports fields; immaculate little station platforms; ordered brick houses painted in colours that would have looked garish in the city but that looked merely cheerful here; grove after grove of coconut trees; an occasional stream or backwater. And ever so suddenly, like a flash of benediction, a view of the open sea, separated from my train only by a thin ribbon of land.

Mangalore seemed sleepy when I got off the train, and it seemed sleepy when I left my hotel in search of lunch. I was to learn, over the course of my days there, that it was a town that seemed sleepy right through the week, as if just walking its rolling, undulating streets rocked its residents into drowsiness. Its restaurants displayed such a pleasing lack of business drive that they seemed almost anachronistic. One restaurant that I spotted, called Hotel Kudla, had used the excuse of ongoing roadwork in the area to down shutters indefinitely—even though the restaurant's front door remained perfectly accessible.

I walked around for half an hour, looking for a place to eat, before the February sun began to feel more uncomfortable than warm. My usual markers weren't working in Mangalore. I tried to peek into restaurants to see if I could spot groups of locals, but every dining hall was uniformly empty. I pondered the names of the restaurants, trying to figure out whether they sounded generically touristy or specifically Mangalorean, but I got nowhere with that either. Finally, out of a desperate desire for shade, I ducked into a building, descended a flight of fire-escape stairs, and in the basement of the Hotel Dakshin, I ordered my first fish curry in Mangalore.

I had come to Mangalore expecting to fall completely in love with its fish curry, but I lusted instead, for much of my time there, after another dish, before I rediscovered my original love on the very morning of my departure. I had eaten the signature curry only once before, years ago, and I remember being entranced by its silky gravy, smooth and deep orange and full of flavour—very much the opposite, in fact, of Kerala's toddy shop *meen* curry, which was pungent and overwhelming, and which broke apart into its oil and non-oil layers upon standing for even a few seconds. To my palate, the Mangalore curry was the superior one, and I expected this to be a joyful reunion.

But it didn't begin well, or perhaps my hopes were set too high. That first curry—turmeric-yellow from a certain angle, red from chilli powder from another—was watery and bland. In the middle of the dish, like an algae-covered rock jutting out of the sea, was a hump of bangda, or mackerel, glinting a silvery green under the light. Mackerel has a famously insistent taste, but this fish was shy and reclusive, as if it would have rather been at home with a good book. I hacked at it from various angles, but it remained dull and uncooperative.

A possible reason revealed itself when I was presented with the bill: Rs 10 for the curry, and another Rs 10 for the dosa I had ordered with it. What kind of fish curry—in this day and age, in a restaurant in a prosperous town—cost Rs 10? I feared the answer. I'd read too much about how quickly mackerel spoiled, and about the scombroid food poisoning that followed rapidly, with its retinue of symptoms: dizziness, rashes, nausea, blurred vision. For the first time in my life, I put down a 50 per cent tip, because I had no smaller notes or coins. My mind reeling, and already feeling faintly ill in my imagination, I left the Hotel Dakshin and walked a dejected kilometre or so. Then, deciding that perhaps another meal would work as some consolation, I entered an eatery called Nihals, sat down, and called weakly for the fish of the day.

More bangda curry arrived, with a serving of coarse red rice and a side of curried potato. But now things were looking up. The mackerel tasted fresher, although still not as distinctive as I expected it to be; its bath of gravy was smoother, speckled with mustard seeds and a whisper of ginger, but it still wasn't as fierce as I wanted it. Recalling Liebling's thesis of fieldwork opportunities, I ordered a bangda masala fry (garlic and coconut; crisped; skin blistered and peeling off like that of a banana; very good) and ate my way through this second lunch. When the bill came—Rs 42, which included Rs 30 for the fry—I began to understand and feel better about Mangalore's prices. If anything, Hotel Dakshin had overcharged me.

Emerging into a mellower late afternoon sun, I wandered aimlessly down the road, turning into smaller alleys, and passing marketplaces that had yet to reopen for the day. But everywhere I went, I saw unfamiliar restaurants with worn signboards, each impassive in its appeal and yet taunting me with unknown promise. The best Mangalore fish curry in the world could have come out of any of those kitchens, but with my trial-and-error technique of random walkabout, I ran the very substantial risk of never finding it. At that juncture, and with a Hotel Dakshin behind me, the thought was too frightening to bear. Pulling out my cell phone, I began to call around for assistance.

Mangalore lies on a curve of land that descends from the Western Ghats to the sea, and it is deeply enamoured of its waters—the backwaters of the Netravati and Gurupura rivers, but also the coast, where waves wash up tiredly and rest a while before leaping on their return journey towards Arabia. In his book *In An Antique Land,* Amitav Ghosh describes the 'great palm-fringed lagoon, lying tranquil under a quicksilver sky,' joined to the ocean only by a narrow channel of water. Mangalore's glorious stretches of sand were its first ports, inviting boats that could be beached safely. In the Middle Ages, to the Arabian traveller who had never left home before, it must have been an awesome sight: pristine sands, lavish vegetation, a rich entry into a vast new land.

On my way to Panambur Beach, Mahesh, my auto-rickshaw driver, happened to ask me where I was from.

'Madras,' I said. (I've never quite been able to call the city by its new name, even though it was renamed Chennai just one year after I began living there. I've often wondered at that inability. Either it is evidence of a buried conservative streak, or a liberal sense that scoffs at the inadequate rationale behind the change of the name. Or maybe it is simply the very flimsy conceit that a real, dyed-in-the-wool Madrasi would never call his city Chennai, and that I fancy my wool to be as dyed as they come.)

At any rate, I said: 'Madras.'

'Ah, Madras,' Mahesh said, and drove peaceably along for another half kilometre. Then: 'I've been there once, you know.'

By this time, I had been away from home for over two weeks, and I was beginning to miss it. I would have grabbed at any opportunity to talk about Madras.

'Oh? When was this?'

'Seven years ago,' he replied. Just a few hours before he arrived in the city, Mahesh explained, the chief minister at the time, J. Jayalalithaa, had arrested the opposition leader, M. Karunanidhi, in a dramatic nocturnal operation. Consequently, Karunanidhi's party had organized a city-wide protest strike, and buses and local trains weren't running. 'The strike was beginning just as I got off the train,' Mahesh said. 'I had to finally take an auto-rickshaw all the way to my destination, Padi. It cost me Rs 120.' After a minute, delightfully oblivious of all irony, he said: 'These auto drivers always fleece you.'

Panambur Beach is a dozen kilometres north of Mangalore, just past a giant port that ships out, among other things, iron ore from the Kudremukh mines. A beach festival had concluded the previous day, and all its paraphernalia—balloon-shooting stalls, food stations, rusty little carousel rides, banners—still stood, unmanned and desolate in the setting sun, like a graveyard of amusement. To one side was a giant billboard that morbidly advertised the number of swimmers who had died at Panambur each year, thereby cautioning visitors to stay on the sands. It seemed to deter nobody; the beach was filled with swimmers towelling off, or still dripping, or emerging from the surf laughing and playfully flicking water at each other.

Mangalore's open shoreline has been, in a way, the making of its particularly complex strain of cuisine. Already it is jostled, on either side, by two prominent cooking schools—the Malayali, to its south, and the Konkan, to its north. Then there is the food of its indigenous Bunt community and of the newly converted Christians who fled the Goan Inquisition when it began, in 1560, to suspect them of relapsing into their old faiths. Arab traders, settling in Mangalore as well as further down the Malabar Coast, brought their own culinary preferences—what has come to be called Moplah cuisine, with its meat-intensive biryanis and curries.

Which of these distinctive worlds of cooking is responsible for the rawa fry, I am not entirely sure. In all probability, they melded together like genetically superior parents and produced this stunner of a dish. When I was lured away from my search for the perfect fish curry, it was the rawa fry that seduced me—more often than not a ladyfish, or kane, coated with a patina of spice and a sheath of grainy semolina, and then fried into a golden-brown, crunchy segment of heaven.

I ate my first rawa fry at Mesha, an eatery commended highly, in my interrogations of Mangalorean friends, for its food that tasted of home. Appropriately then, Mesha resides in a small, old house near the New Chitra Theatre, so unobtrusive that, in the dark, feeling a little like Theseus in his labyrinth, I wandered down multiple wrong lanes before chancing accidentally upon the right one. In a string of unlit houses, Mesha's tiny windows were the only ones resplendent with light. In the living room, floored with red oxide and roofed with fat rafters, there were two big tables and a narrow wooden bench that reminded me of school; just beyond was another room with another table and then the kitchen, clearly in my line of sight. I was the only customer there. Mesha's staff had taken strategic positions of lethargy around the living room, all watching a cricket match with Kannada commentary on a diminutive television—a match that was so evidently of the grassroots, sub-junior variety that I was surprised it was even being televised.

The cricket can't have been very gripping, because when I began to ask questions about my food, Mesha's waiters clustered around me to provide helpful, but sometimes contradictory, answers. In a few seconds, they reached a consensus that the chutney accompanying the rawa fry was made of tomato and a little tamarind, but the debate raged longer over how the fish was prepared. One section of the house argued that the layer of spice contained a little egg and flour to bind it to the fish, while the other maintained that there was no egg or flour, and that it was just an ordinary mixture of spices.

Finally, one of the members of the second set disappeared into the kitchen, and in the absence of a quorum, the debate stalled momentarily and eyes started to drift back to the television. Two minutes later, our emissary returned, and in a remarkably bipartisan gesture, admitted that his party was wrong, and that egg and flour were both very much present. The bill was successfully passed. Then a businesslike gentleman, who must have been the chairman of the appropriations committee, cut in to ask if I wanted to order anything else.

I most definitely did. I asked for rice and a curry, which arrived in a shallow saucer, inflammatory with kokum but still somehow smooth with coconut, so deeply ruddy that I was certain it included tomatoes. (I was wrong. I'd learn later that Mangaloreans used tomatoes in chicken and mutton dishes, but rarely when they curried fish.) The parliament around me rattled off the other ingredients: ginger, long green chillies, garlic, onions, and fenugreek. The cut of fish, they admitted, was just of a cheap river fish, to inject the gravy with some sort of flavour. I'm pretty sure they told me exactly what that fish was, but I was too busy eating to pay them my fullest attention.

The fish in the rawa fry was what they called '*murumeen*', a Malayalam word that refers to a type of snapper found in estuaries and seasonally in the lower reaches of rivers. Under its crust of rawa, it was soft and flaky, and hit with citrus from the lemon juice in the spice paste. If I did it right, I could peel off all three layers— the crunchy rawa, the tangy spice, the delicate fish—at the same time, to then assemble them in my mouth in an explosive fusion of textures and tastes. I picked the murumeen clean, spooned the last of the curry into my mouth, and sat back on my schoolroom bench to watch the rest of the cricket match. From outside, as the night deepened, we must have looked like a home-grown version of Edward Hopper's *Nighthawks*, sitting silently in this glowing old house that opened onto the resounding stillness of Mangalore.

All my frantic telephoning, on my first day in town, had fortuitously led me to Jaideep Shenoy, a correspondent of the *Hindu* in Mangalore, a stolid, laconic individual who was kind enough to take a few hours out of a working day to listen to the woes of a directionless eater. To Shenoy, I owe thanks on two counts: For accompanying me to Narayan's, and for introducing me to Vasudev Boloor.

First, Narayan's—a tiny restaurant, sitting inside an alley near Mangalore's riverside wharf. The area itself is called Bunder, the word surviving intact from the Persian term for 'port' or, more poetically, 'haven.' (Shenoy's guide to finding the restaurant is more prosaic: Go to the State Bank of India building, and then just ask for Narayan's. 'Anybody can tell you.') At lunchtime, Narayan's has a teeming ground floor and, via a narrow staircase, service on the first floor as well. Even from the doorway, I could see straight through the dining hall into the kitchen, where a stone grinder of Olympian proportions churned out vast quantities of fresh masala. Around tables that were already occupied, waiting patrons stood like tussocks of patient grass. Every so often, they were nudged to one side or the other with a murmured 'Side-u, side-u' from the owner of Narayan's, who circulated with a big tray of fish fresh from the kitchen.

The specialty of Narayan's, Shenoy told me, was its tawa-fried fish-fillets of seer and ladyfish or whole sardines and mackerel that have been fried on a flat, hot pan. But that is not quite accurate. Narayan's specialty is the masala that is slapped onto that fried fish as it sizzles on the pan, the masala that I could see writhing out of the stone grinder, the masala that dusted the fish and otherwise aggregated in fried lumps on the circulating tray like spicy, red snowdrifts. Shyam Sunder, the owner, would solicitously bend over a table, and a customer would say, through a full mouth, 'Kane' perhaps or 'Bangda,' but then he would rake the tray with a sharp eye and point to those crisp nuggets of masala. 'That too, please.'

Shyam Sunder's father started Narayan's sixty years ago, and it has since become an institution of tawa-fried delight in Mangalore. It passes with flying colours the popularly understood test for a good restaurant in India—that its food must be so good, and so cheap, that auto-rickshaw drivers and wealthy businessmen set aside their backgrounds to eat at the same table. On traditional steel thalis, waiters set down rice, pickle, a curried vegetable and some fish gravy, but nobody begins to eat until the almighty tray has blessed the plate with fish.

A tawa fry is rarely oily; instead, the crusted masala coats the fish fillet almost as if it were protecting the soft, white meat inside. The masala here was indescribably good. It was fried enough to suggest its immense potential as a meal all by itself, but it also lifted strong flavours out of the fish, like a coach goading verve out of a champion athlete. Shenoy didn't bother with the rice and the vegetable at all, and I followed his example. After an initial piece of seer each, we commandeered the tray and lifted sardines (naturally oily, and very moist) and ladyfish (dry, but redeemed entirely by extra masala) onto our plates. Then, when we could eat no more, I stood next to the kitchen for a few minutes, simply sniffing at the frying masala on the tawa, deep-breathing fanatically, trying to fill my lungs with enough aroma to last the day.

Down the road from Narayan's, a short walk made considerably longer by a full belly, was the wharf, crammed that afternoon with boats moored three rows deep, so thickly clustered that you could have walked on their decks from one end of the pier to the other. Across the boats, on the other side of the road, stood a row of small shops offering cold storage facilities, blocks of ice, fishmeal, engine oil and diesel. It was a sweltering afternoon, and particularly soupy and humid by the river; on many boats, the chopped ice being loaded into yellow plastic tubs started melting even before it could be lowered into the holds. In the mornings, fish were hauled out of those same holds and carted up to Mangalore's main fish market—just opposite the State Bank of India building, a few hundred metres away.

A helpful property of the human mind is that it can sense when something is out of place even before it deciphers what specifically is wrong with the picture. At the Mangalore wharf, I experienced the reverse effect; walking around with the dullness of mind that heat and satiation can often induce, I couldn't shake the feeling that something was very right, very familiar, and yet out of place by virtue of that very familiarity. A few minutes passed before the mental tumblers fell into place, one by one: There was Tamil everywhere. The signboards of the shops were in the Tamil script; the boats prows' had Tamil names painted on them, and the fishermen around me were hollering and cursing in Tamil. It felt like an unexpected homecoming, and I had to wait till the next day for Vasudev Boloor to explain it to me.

Vasudev Boloor accumulates bureaucratic titles as a wealthy collector does art—with discrimination and judgement, and with due affection for each individual piece, but nevertheless in great quantities. Boloor is the president of the Mogaveera Vyavasthapaka Mandali, a Mangalore fishermen's cooperative. He is also secretary of the Akhila Karnataka Fishermen's Parishad, which should really make its mind up about which language to use in naming itself. Additionally, he is the secretary of the National Fishworkers' Federation and of the Coastal Karnataka Fishermen Action Committee. All these may or may not be essentially the same organization; one can well imagine a Borges short story in which a grand conclave of all the various federations results in the discovery that they are all really composed of the same members.

I met Boloor first when Shenoy took me to Roshni Nilaya, a school of social work, and dragged him out of a meeting he was chairing. Boloor is a short, balding man with a wise face, intelligent eyes that shine even through the thickest of spectacles, and skin that is coloured and creased like a walnut. One of his fingers is permanently out of joint, broken (he would tell me later) during a student protest in Mysore; his fellow agitators included J. H. Patel and S. Bangarappa, future chief ministers of Karnataka.

Boloor, Shenoy and I sat in the Roshni Nilaya canteen, over plastic cups of awful tea, and Boloor told me about the Tamilian fishermen who had begun to migrate in large numbers to the Konkan Coast. Then he told me about how Mangalore's own fishing community had withdrawn from the profession. 'At the College of Fisheries here in Mangalore, all the students are from outside Karnataka,' he said. 'They're the ones who learn the science behind the fishing—fish diseases, weather patterns, that kind of thing.' Then, perhaps somehow reminded of the meeting that was languishing without his stewardship, he tossed back his tea and asked if I would come to his house the next morning, to talk at further length.

Boloor lives in a neat brick bungalow in a quiet Mangalore locality that is also called Boloor; whether the area is named after the clan or vice versa, I could not ascertain. I reached early, so I waited in the living room until Boloor, still bare-torso'd and swathed in an enormous white dhoti, finished his prayers and came out to join me.

When he was a boy, living on an island near the Tipu Sultan Bathery, Boloor would go fishing before school (and later, before college) every day. 'My father was a fisherman, so I'd do what I could to help him and then leave for school,' he said. Wading into the river, he would reel out a large net and then try to scare fish into it, a technique that he said was called—and here he made a lovely, deep, gobbling sound—'bolupu'. 'My father and I would unload all our fish at Bunder, and while my mother would take the catch to the fish market to sell, I'd run for class.'

But Boloor's love for officialdom soon began to interfere with his love for fishing. When he was in school, he joined the Rashtriya Seva Dal, which gathered the sons and daughters of fishermen into a juvenile union of sorts. 'We met weekly for debates, and we would campaign to publicize the difficulties of fishing families,' Boloor said, with the pride of a mother in her first-born. In college, he majored in active protest, including that Mysore agitation of finger-breaking intensity. When he started working at the Karnataka Electricity Board, sure enough, he promptly set up the first KEB Employees Union. Only after his retirement from the KEB did Boloor accept the various honorary positions in the various fishing bodies, merging his penchant for organizing people with his roots in the fishing community.

Boloor asked me where in Mangalore I had eaten, and as if I'd entered a confession booth, I told him about my impromptu love affair with the rawa fry, but also rather defensively about my inability to find the Mangalore fish curry as I remembered it. 'That's not surprising,' Boloor said, and orated a little on the declining quality of fish in general. 'But you should know better, after all. The best Mangalore fish curry is not made in restaurants but in homes.' Having said that, without any ado, he led me out of the living room, across his front yard and through a gate in the compound wall, into the house next door. 'This is my brother's son's wife, Shailaja,' he said, introducing me to a beautiful young woman in an orange-red salwar-kameez, her long hair tied into a bun, still wet from her morning bath. 'She'll make you some fish curry right now.'

My desperate reluctance to impose had no effect. Boloor went back into his house to complete some work, while Shailaja brought two large mackerel out of her house and began to cut and de-scale them on a curved blade, sitting by a well in the courtyard. She removed the innards of the fish, wrenched their jaws off, cut them rapidly into thick fillets, and washed them with well water, making conversation all the while. 'I've been making this curry since I was a teenager, when I learned it from my mother,' she said. 'And we make it at home every day. There's almost no meal without it.'

In her kitchen, with its sloping roof and its blue and orange walls, Shailaja showed me the huge tub of masala that she made afresh every two or three days, and the tins of ingredients that went into the masala. 'For every coconut, there are thirty-five to forty dried chillies, a tablespoon of turmeric, a handful of coriander seeds, a fistful of tamarind, and some cumin and fenugreek and mustard seeds and salt,' she recited, the measurements getting more inexact as she progressed. 'You fry everything except the coconut, and then you grind it all into this paste.'

Shailaja scooped up a few handfuls of the masala, thick and bright orange like clay, and mixed it into some water in a pot until it flowed off her hands with the consistency of thick tomato soup. How did she know how much she needed? I asked. 'The hand knows,' she said, with a smile that made my knees wobble. Expertly, she cut and added some ginger and three long, green chillies to the pot, and then some salt. On one of the stove's two burners, the gravy began to simmer, throwing clouds of heat into the tiny kitchen. Our foreheads erupted in honest sweat. Behind Shailaja, her mother-in-law stood with a toothy grin and eyes that watched and weighed every step of the process. Just outside, in the living room, the television was going berserk with commentary about a Sanath Jayasuriya fusillade in an India-Sri Lanka cricket match.

Eight minutes later, when the surface of the curry started to resemble bubbling lava, Shailaja slipped the fillets down the sides of the pot into the gravy. 'Don't stir the curry with a ladle, because that'll break the fish,' she warned. Instead, she grabbed the rim of the pot with a cloth and gently shook it around. Really enraged now, the curry began to spit out hot little flecks into the air. With a spoon, Shailaja dabbed a little curry onto her palm and tasted it, and then she added another twist of salt, shook the pot once more, and turned off the stove. The entire operation, from gutting the fish to finishing off the curry, had taken roughly twenty minutes.

And that was how, on the morning of my departure, sitting on a small kitchen stool with a large bowl in my hands, with the television still audible and with Shailaja and her mother-in-law watching me with round eyes, I fell back in love with the Mangalore fish curry (and also, I must admit, fell temporarily in love with its chef). The heat of those thirty-five to forty dried chillies rampaged through my sinuses and made my nose run, but in an odd way, the mackerel tamed that heat—so much, in fact, that I imagined I could feel past the heat and pick out every individual spice. The mackerel, fresh and firm, came away easily in big, moist flakes, and I rolled each bite around in its gorgeous, fiery bath before eating it. On its way down, the curry scalded my mouth, seared my tonsils, and sent parades of flavour marching up and down my tongue. The most perfect rawa fry could have danced itself off the plate and in front of my eyes at that moment, and I wouldn't have accorded it a second glance.

On my way out, I stopped again at Boloor's house to thank him. He was leaving home as well, and as we walked to the gate together, I filled his ears with praise of Shailaja's fish curry. 'Really, that good, was it?' Boloor asked. 'But then, I wouldn't know,' he went on, this stalwart president of the Mogaveera Vyavasthapaka Mandali and secretary of the Akhila Karnataka Fishermen's Parishad, of the National Fishworkers' Federation and of the Coastal Karnataka Fishermen Action Committee. 'You see, I don't eat fish.'

6
On pursuing the fastest fish in the ocean

Like all fishermen, Danny Moses best remembers the one that got away.

A few years ago, Moses was angling on the Angria Bank, a huge submerged coral reef, more than a hundred kilometres from his home state of Goa. Around three in the afternoon, when a day at sea is at its most deliciously torpid, Moses' big lure suddenly popped. 'The fish bit and then it just kept diving,' Moses remembers. 'It was just a small reel, so we were a little scared. But we were sure it was a marlin, trying to go deep and throw us off as they usually do.'

After a few pregnant minutes, though, the fish modified its battle plan. Rocketing to the surface, it performed a complete somersault at some distance from the boat; only when it repeated the cartwheel at closer quarters did Moses recognize it as a sailfish, one of the most elusive, mighty quarries of the deep-sea angler. 'We could see the lure snagged at the corner of its mouth,' he says. 'It was shaking its head so violently that the rod was whipping about from side to side—thaap! thaap! thaap!'

The sailfish fought Moses every second of the ninety minutes he took to reel it closer to his boat. Then, putting on his gloves, Moses began pulling in the braided shock-leader line, hand over hand, inch by arduous inch. 'It was seven or eight feet long, and probably fifty kilogrammes in weight. Its fin alone was two-and-a-half feet high,' he says. 'We were fishing on a catch-and-release basis, so all I needed to do was to touch and tag the fish to claim it as a catch.'

But sometimes, Moses admits ruefully, the size of a fish can just freeze you. When the sailfish was three feet from the boat, Moses found himself staring right into its rolling, furious eyes. 'He was going gold and purple with rage, and these huge black bands were running down his side,' he says. 'The sailfish's bill is like a razor—you put your hand out, and you might get it sliced off. That was the dilemma.' And in that moment of indecision, Moses panicked. 'I decided not to reach out.'

It takes a lot to push Moses into panic. He is a big man with powerful arms and shoulders, and like many Goans, he has been an inveterate angler for almost all of his life; even his keychain is a fluorescent yellow fishing lure. I had heard much about his vast experience with game fish, and when I met him, Moses gifted me this weighty thought: 'My son fishes because I fish; I fish because my father fished, and that's how it's always been here.' For the better part of two decades now, he has worked runs out to sea with sport-fishing clients, out of the states of Goa and Maharashtra, acquiring a formidable knowledge of the waters and their fish. But on that day, the sailfish froze Moses. 'I've tried to justify it to myself so many times since then,' he says. 'Maybe at the time, I was still a little green when it came to sailfish. But I flunked. There's no two ways about that.'

By the standards of the Indo-Pacific sailfish, or the *Istiophorus platypterus*, Moses' adversary wasn't even particularly a monster. A really hefty sailfish can weigh as much as a hundred kilogrammes and stretch over three-and-a-half metres from rapier-like bill to muscular tail. On its back, like the eponymous sails of a grand schooner, is a black, ribbed dorsal fin, sometimes taller even than the body's own width. 'When you spot one, it's a real sight, particularly in the dark,' Moses tells me. 'You just see the head and the bill first. Then, under the boat's lights, you can see through the water, which is as clear as glass, and its fin begins to unfold and rise ominously.'

All that monstrous bulk can also move frighteningly fast. In the 1920s, a series of experiments attempted to put a number on a sailfish's speed by measuring the length of fishing line it pulled from a reel. The stopwatch clicked into action, and in three seconds, the sailfish ran away with ninety metres of line. That brings its top clocked speed in the region of a hundred and ten kilometres per hour and makes it the fastest fish in the ocean. Approaching its top pace, the sailfish folds its sail down flat into a groove along its back, like a captain stowing his sheets and starting up the outboard motor.

Even more spectacularly, the sailfish can change colour in an instant, going from its usual dull gray to a regal mix of shimmering silver, blue, purple and gold. On its skin, cells called melanophores, containing dark deposits of pigments, can make themselves transparent. Underneath, like a buried vein of precious gems, is another layer of cells named iridophores, which break and reflect light into an explosion of colours. This neat prismatic trick, said Peter Baptista, a fervent angler from Mumbai, explains the local moniker of the sailfish: the *mor maach*, or the peacock fish.

Baptista, a grandfatherly man who used to be a corporate executive in New Delhi, retired and returned to Mumbai in 1993 with the express purpose of spending his days golfing and fishing. His family originally hailed from Goa as well; in fact, a common acquaintance had directed me to both him and Moses. Baptista has wrested sport fish out of rivers since 1966, but for the last fifteen years, even as his hair has thinned and whitened, he has taken on the more ferocious game of the ocean. 'When I came back to Mumbai, I wanted to start angling in the sea,' Baptista says. 'But everything I'd learned over forty years in the rivers— none of that held any good in salt water.' So he started over and worked diligently at his fishing, until he was yanking marlin and tuna and barracuda effortlessly out of the sea.

It was Baptista who first told me about the sailfish, and about its uncannily precise annual visit to the Indian coastline. For much of the year, the sailfish is found in deeper seas, or at reefs like the Angria Bank, which is at least twenty metres deep. 'They're predator fish, and they hunt like packs of wolves,' Moses says. 'The small fish swim in underwater currents, so the sailfish wait on the edge of these currents, dart in, grab their food, and dart back out.' With their threatening profiles, the sailfish will often herd terrified sardines into a dense cloud and then batter their prey into submission with their long bills. It's a complex, almost military way to get dinner.

In September, however, as the monsoon's rains recede and smaller fish like the flathead mullet make their way down the rivers into the sea, the sailfish makes an excursion of fifteen to twenty days into estuarial waters in search of food. Those are possibly its easiest meals of the year. If the oceanic currents are conveyor belts of intermittent, rapidly moving batches of food, the estuaries are groaning buffet tables of mackerel, sardines and mullet.

The year I went sailfishing, that twenty-day window opened right in the middle of September, on the day that Hindus ritually immerse their clay idols of Ganesha in the sea. (Baptista always uses festivals for his calculations. 'Somehow,' he says, 'the Hindu calendar is amazingly precise about changes of currents. It's like clockwork.') But out at sea, the weather was still rough, and sporadic gusts of rain were still pounding the western coast. Baptista had agreed to take me on a sailfish expedition, but on the weekend we'd planned to depart, I flew down to Mumbai from my home in New Delhi, only to learn that a new squall had set in. I flew back home, and we waited another impatient week, hoping that the weather would turn before our narrow window closed on us.

When the skies cleared, we headed down the Konkan Coast, to a little town between Mumbai and Goa. I'm going to call it Xanadu, because anglers, as a species, are obsessively secretive about the location of their favourite waters, and because Baptista knew from a previous trip that Xanadu's coast was a rich mine for sailfish. This habit of secrecy is as old as angling itself, and the world today, with its overfished rivers and seas, has retrofitted itself to have that habit make even more sense than before. 'We don't even publish our trip photos on the *Indian Angler* web site,' Baptista said, 'because you can figure out where it's been taken from the view in the background.' I was told the name, I suspect, on a strict need-to-know basis; if I was to get there, I needed to know.

Baptista discovered Xanadu last year, when he was poring over a Wikimapia image of the coast, looking for promising estuarial waters. It is a chubby finger of land, densely wooded, with a creek on one side and the sea on the other; the finger ends where the creek meets the sea. 'We came here last year, but we weren't exactly welcomed by the local fishermen,' Baptista said. 'We had to work to get friendly with these guys. But we're regulars now.'

At false dawn, a little before six in the morning, Baptista, his adult nephews Emil and Yvan Carvalho, and I drove through Xanadu's woods and its clustered hamlets of fishing communities, all wide awake already. Near the mouth of the creek, close to a temple, two local fishermen named Uttam and Kalidas waited for us with the *Vinoba Prasad*—a bright blue, twenty-foot boat with a fitted outboard motor, powerful enough to take us the fifteen kilometres out to sea. Uttam lit a clutch of incense sticks and stuck them into a hole in the prow of the boat. A kilometre out, he would make another offering to the gods of the sea—a coconut, betel nuts and leaves tossed into the water—and circle this once with the boat before chugging further.

As we left the creek, mullet leaped out of the water around us. 'The fish are certainly running,' Baptista said. Just the previous evening, Xanadu's fishermen had deployed a net known as the rampon—a massive, semi-circular net, with either end held fast on shore. By just waiting a few hours and then drawing the rampon net in, they had snagged seven tons of pomfret. 'They're certainly running,' Baptista said again.

Tatters of fog hung over the coast, filtering the dim light unevenly, the patchwork sky like something out of a Turner seascape. There were already other fishing craft in the creek and just outside its mouth; in them, men sat wrapped in shawls, with a solitary line, tied to one of their fingers, leading from their hand into the water. They were so still that they might have been asleep; only occasionally they would jiggle the line to keep their bait moving. Off to the side, one slice of the horizon was a dense sheet of gray. Somewhere, not very far away, it was raining.

Marcel Proust once wrote about the abrupt thrill of a fish breaking the surface of water, comparing it to the flash of a metaphor in prose. The sight of a worthy catch is breathlessly anticipated; the thrill of the sport resides in how suddenly it can turn. But for the rest of the time, the art of fishing is really the art of waiting in thin disguise—waiting not only from hour to hour, as we were doing at sea, or from day to day, as with the fisherman Santiago in Ernest Hemingway's *The Old Man and the Sea*, but even from year to year, as for the annual Indian visitation of the sailfish. There is no room in the boat for impatience; I can't think of any other sport that so effectively screens its participants on the basis of a single quality of temperament.

Big-game fishing in India is one of the British Raj's many persistent legacies, although environmental degradation and conservation laws have now threatened the sport with extinction. For years, the prize catch in India was the golden mahseer, a gleaming river fish that British anglers used to call the Indian salmon. The mahseer can be huge; in 1870, in a book titled *Thirteen Years Amongst the Wild Beasts of India*, an Englishman named G. P. Sanderson claimed to have once caught a one-hundred-and-thirty-pound monster. But the population of the mahseer has now dwindled in many Indian rivers, and angling for it is sharply restricted.

Thus constrained on the rivers, many sport-fishing enthusiasts turned increasingly to India's coast, vying with commercial fishermen for the tuna, shark, marlin, sailfish and barracuda that lay in the waters. 'But even at sea, overfishing is becoming a problem,' Baptista said. Massive trawlers scrape the bottom of the seabed to pluck every possible fish into their holds, wrecking the ocean's ecology and scooping in worthless fry before the small fish can mature into adults. In such conditions, the post-monsoon blooms of fish become bonanzas, for fishermen as well as predatory fish.

In the *Vinoba Prasad*, Emil had already bolted black metal stocks to the gunwale and to the boat's benches, to help hold the rods steady. The fishermen then assembled their fibreglass rods, heavy in the hand, with smooth reel locking mechanisms that purred satisfyingly as they let their line go. 'In estuaries, with all the underwater rocks, there is a greater danger of abrasion to the line,' Baptista had told me earlier. 'So we use a really strong microdynamic reel—made of the same stuff they use to make bullet-proof vests. You put a finger to that line when a sailfish is dragging it at top speed, and it will just get lopped off.' At the end of the line was a lure known as the Giant Trembler—a silvery fish-shaped object, about four inches long, with twin three-pronged hooks, glinting odd colours in the uncertain light. The lure was filled with ball bearings, Yvan told me. In the water, it would vibrate and make an intriguing enough sound for a predator fish to take a second look at this strange new snack.

We were barely on our way when we hooked our first catch. One rod had been loosely resting in its stock, and Yvan was just beginning to cinch it in when it leapt out of his hands; a few seconds earlier, and the rod would have been in the water.

The rod jerked back and forth, and Yvan puffed as he sought to stay in control. 'Emil, get the belt around him,' Baptista shouted. Emil, scrambling from his seat, picked up a white belt with a large plastic buckle, used by the standing fisherman to brace the rod against his belly as he played the fish (or as the fish played him).

'Get the belt on him, Emil,' Baptista hollered again.

'I'm trying, Uncle, but he's too fat,' Emil hollered back, laughing. He paid out a few more lengths of belt, looped it right over Yvan's bulky fishing jacket, and pulled it tight. Yvan himself was largely unaware of this exchange as he peered into the sea, as if he were willing the fish to submit.

It turned out to be a golden trevally, a yellow tropical fish that had been trailing in the boat's wake and that had received a hook in the corner of its mouth for its troubles. The trevally had fought as trevallies usually do—by presenting its flat side to the direction it was being pulled in, to create as much resistance as possible. 'A trevally to open your season, Yvan,' Emil said. 'That's not bad.' Yvan shrugged.

We continued to seek more open waters. To the east, the skies were beginning to flare with the first approach of dawn, and the

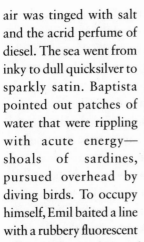

air was tinged with salt and the acrid perfume of diesel. The sea went from inky to dull quicksilver to sparkly satin. Baptista pointed out patches of water that were rippling with acute energy— shoals of sardines, pursued overhead by diving birds. To occupy himself, Emil baited a line with a rubbery fluorescent yellow-and-green lure and threw it into the ocean to attract squid.

Orbiting an old lighthouse, waiting for a sailfish to bite

We were headed, eventually, to a sprinkling of rocky islets rising out of the sea, the biggest of them sporting a stubby lighthouse that looked abandoned but wasn't, and some houses that looked abandoned and were, in fact, abandoned. 'Here, there are more rocks under the water, and some of the bait fish tend to hide beneath them,' Baptista said. The predator fish often swam these waters, poking under the rocks to rustle their prey out. Gunning the motor down, we began making slow, laborious sorties around the islets, the three fishermen hunched over their rods, staring into the sea.

As if even sparring with a sailfish was an honour, many fishermen tell proud stories of their defeats in the battle with the monster at the end of their line, as Moses did with me. Participating in the extended sailfish mythos is sufficient in itself, and a mythos it has certainly become. In his memoir, *The Sailfish and the Sacred Mountain*, Will Johnson describes the sailfish as 'a Neptunian being unequaled in majesty and evasiveness, a watery version of the Himalayan snow leopard.' To actually catch one is closer to a benediction than a feat of skill. A veteran could fish his entire life without even spotting a sailfish, and a rookie could pull one in on his very first trip to sea, as Johnson says he did in the Florida Keys.

Even a lost battle can often be spectacular. When it is snared, the sailfish leaps out of the water and, fully upright, propels itself across the surface solely on the strength of its thrashing tail, just as a dolphin does. The dolphin appears to do it, though, out of some sense of self-conscious cuteness; with the sailfish, it's all outrage and menace. Veteran anglers call it 'tailwalking,' and they will tell stories—often ones that sound, quite literally, incredible—of how a sailfish tailwalked around their boat for an hour or more

So luminous is the prestige inherent in catching a sailfish, not to mention the attendant bragging rights, that any claim of having landed one can be met with automatic suspicion and doubt. The Sailfish Cup, held in Miami every year, offers a purse of $100,000 to the team that catches and releases the most sailfish over two days, and not unusually, teams must submit video recordings of each catch. What is unusual is the subsequent, very stark stipulation: 'All winning teams will be subject to and must pass polygraph testing. Refusal to take the test will result in disqualification . . . Polygraph tests will include but will not be limited to questions on angling and release procedures and species of fish.' In Miami, the sailfish has to be earned twice over, with the rod and then with the lie-detector; and the second test of nerves is just as wracking as the first.

On the *Vinoba Prasad*, the sun began to beat down more strongly upon our boating party. Uttam steered consistent circles. I thought of breakfast; then, when the water got a little choppier, I tried not to think of breakfast. Every twenty minutes, Emil asked Uttam to slow down, slipped an electronic Fishing Buddy depth finder into the water, and took sonar readouts of the terrain below. 'The mackerel are in,' Baptista said. 'The big fish should be in by now.'

A few minutes after he said that, something bit heavily into his lure.

Few human moves suggest the rapid transformation of potential energy into kinetic energy more than that of the fisherman who has finally felt a tug on his line. Baptista stood suddenly to attention, pushed his hat back on his head to see better, and began the rocking motion that is so familiar to anglers—lean back and pull on the rod, then lean forward to hurriedly retrieve more reel. Emil and Yvan hastily pulled their lines in to avoid entangling them with Baptista's and then started to shout incoherent encouragement. Even Uttam, who had till now kept himself coolly detached from the success or failure of this expedition, appeared to develop a degree of interest in the contest at hand, expectorating once over the side of the boat before putting his chin in his hands to watch the fight.

Many metres from the boat, the fish began to struggle for its life. It fought in one spot for a while and then began to swim furiously around the boat, swinging all the way from Baptista's left to his right and forcing him to pivot where he stood. At that distance, there was still no way of knowing what fish it was, but its size and power were on obvious display. It was too late for Baptista to strap on his belt, so he painfully braced the end of the rod against his belly instead. The line whistled a shrill, ragged tune as it cut through the water around us.

For nearly ten minutes, Baptista and his fish continued their tug of war, but it was slowly becoming apparent that he had succeeded in working his opponent closer to the boat. Emil grabbed a big net and prepared to help pull the fish in. Baptista, sweating now from the heat and the exertion and the fever of the hunt, paused for a moment as the fish approached the prow of the boat, and we all leaned eagerly over the edge to peer into the water. It was, quite unmistakably, a huge grouper.

With its mottled skin and bulbous mouth, the grouper is one of the more ugly residents of the ocean, looking uncannily like a boxer with a damaged face and a permanent fat lip. It is also a perfectly respectable catch for sport fishermen. While they aren't very fast fish, they can be large and shrewd, diving powerfully into the refuge of rocks in the hope of shredding the line that holds them. Landing a grouper is a victory of brute strength, and it is ordinarily a satisfactory trophy—but not if you've really been after a prize like the sailfish.

Some of the spirit seemed to leak out of the *Vinoba Prasad* after the grouper was hauled on board. We made a few more revolutions around the lighthouse, and then again around another knot of rocks nearby. Yvan caught a yellowtail, but this only appeared to depress the party further.

After another hour, we headed back towards the coast to trawl the mouth of the creek. Moses had mentioned to me that sailfish sometimes enter the river system in search of food, and he had told me a story of a particularly greedy one that had swum up the River Mandovi in Goa, where it was caught by a lucky fisherman. But the Xanadu creek showed no signs of any lurking sailfish. Baptista caught two red snappers in shallower waters with minimal excitement. Yvan snagged a plastic bag.

At half past noon, we called off the great sailfish hunt. When the boat slid into position at a roughly improvised dock, hands reached out to help unload the grouper, and Kalidas squatted at the river's edge to gut the fish immediately. Yvan and Emil began stowing the tackle in the car. Baptista stood silently for a few moments, watching Kalidas at work. Then he shook himself out of his reverie and told me: 'They're saying the water is still cold at the lower depths. Maybe that's the reason the sailfish didn't bite.' But he didn't seem convinced of it himself. 'At least the snapper should make for really good eating,' he said, brightening just a little. In return, I could only offer him the fisherman's eternal consolation—that the sailfish hunt would probably turn out all right next year.

7

On grieving for bygone beaches and fish

I may be wrong, but over the course of two trips to Goa, I formed the distinct impression that its milestones and signboards were doctored. Typically, I would be driving—to Candolim, let us suppose—and a board would announce it to be twenty kilometres away. So I would drive on for another ten minutes, humming along at a consistent 60 kmph, and just when I had calculated that I had driven ten kilometres, another board would pop up, bearing the taunt: 'Candolim: 15 km.' Then I would drive a little faster, and in another ten minutes, when I had recouped enough confidence in my mental arithmetic to be sure of seeing a single-digit reading soon, a smug milestone by the side of the road would flash by: 'Candolim: 12 km.' At this point, invariably, I would begin to feel like I was trapped in a real-world engineering of Zeno's paradox, forever halving the distance to my destination but never quite getting there.

In some cases, such as my harum-scarum pelt to the airport on my second trip, to catch my flight out, this dilation of distances can prove unnerving, particularly if the ticket in your hand is a non-refundable one. But if your flight isn't leaving in forty minutes, or if where you're headed is instead just your third beach of the day, these episodes of understatement could have the opposite effect. Take it easy, the signboards soothingly say, you're not that far away. I can see how this would play into Goa's grander scheme of things, its relentless objective to chill you out.

Goa's is an economy of idleness—not an economy made up of idle people, but an economy that relies on the human desire to idle. To idle is to linger, and to linger is to buy more stuff, eat more stuff and do more stuff on jet-skis: Thence, the Goan economy. But putting that theory into practice is trickier than it sounds, even if, as a state, you can claim to be an idler's paradise by virtue of being endowed with what seems from the air like roughly a million acres of beach. It is not easy to convince people—or, to be anthropologically precise, tourists—that there isn't a better shop or a spicier chicken xacuti or a sleeker jet-ski just around the bend of the road, that they shouldn't be hurrying themselves from sport to sport to banish their regrets. Goa has, by and large, mastered that art of persuasion, but it has had to steamroller a few victims along its determined path to the idylls of tourism.

That list of unfortunates includes fishing, an activity that has for some centuries been a staple Goan pastime, a subsistence profession as well as a flourishing local industry. It is a simple matter, nearly anywhere on the Indian coast, to turn to the person next to you and spark a conversation about fish as food. Only in Goa, however, is it as simple to talk about the act of fishing itself. As if by some vast, ordained consensus, Goans told me, time after time and in the same words: 'Fishing is in our blood.' They sketched for me bucolic visions of the Goan villager stepping out of her hut, her son and daughter by her side and rustic rods in their hands, to spend a quiet evening by the river. One person called fishing 'the only activity that truly cuts across every Goan religion and caste.' Another described his boyhood to be of the sort that I thought existed only in Richmal Crompton books, consisting of muddy boys skipping and fighting their way to the water after school, to fish in homework-less oblivion until sunset. 'Everybody fishes,' I learned during one particularly effusive discussion. 'You need to just sit and watch the complete peace with which these riverfront fishermen fish, to understand why they are so passionate about it.'

I unwittingly gave myself a chance to do that when I arrived an hour early to meet somebody for breakfast in Panaji. It was a fresh morning, the sky scrubbed clean of cloud and a breeze blowing in hesitant gusts from the direction of the ocean. With nothing else to do, I began walking the promenade beside the River Mandovi, a procession of lemon-yellow and powder-blue walls across the road to my right, and moored riverboat casinos with names like *Noah's Ark* and *King's Casino*, dozing after the previous night's excesses, to my left. Just before the road began to climb uphill and turn into a flyover, I came upon a woman leaning upon the white concrete balustrade, looking abstractedly over the river. I stopped a dozen metres away and, remembering that piece of earnest advice, took up my station to watch her fish.

Watching somebody fish is very much like watching somebody stand still. This woman stood, in a white floral shirt and a beige skirt, on sandalled feet, her elbows resting on the balustrade and bearing most of her weight. She wore a fraying straw hat with a narrow brim. She appeared to have passed the age of fifty a few years earlier, but her stocky body looked powerful rather than merely thickened by age, her face was uncreased, and her hair was still a deep matte black. She held a thin wooden pole loosely in her hands, from the end of which an invisible line dropped into the water below; by her feet was a Horlicks bottle containing, I presumed, worms or other bait.

For an angler, she did not seem particularly avid about actually catching anything. Every so often, she joggled her rod, keeping her bait bouncing in the water as if for exercise, but mostly she gazed at the horizon, or off into a copse of trees on the other side of the Mandovi. Once, she changed her bait, pulling up her line, flicking a bedraggled, stringy something off the hook and into the water, and replacing it from the Horlicks bottle with what I now realized was a small hunk of dried fish. A dreamy expression had settled upon her face, so when, half an hour after I had started to watch her, the rod started to writhe in her hands, she looked down with an air of astonishment, as if a fish had swum up to her and begged to be taken home.

A little huffily, she gripped her rod between her knees, as if it were a rail-thin bronco, and began rapidly to pull up her line, hand over hand. The fish came up, and with the line still invisible in the sunlight, it appeared like it was being magically levitated out of the river. It was unidentifiable from where I stood, a flapping pale brown creature half the length of her forearm. After she slid the fish off its hook, she barely glanced at it. Instead, she cocked her arm and lobbed the fish mightily back into the river. Then, appearing annoyed at the interruption, she moodily re-baited her hook, sank it back into the river, and went back to her original stance, propped up by the balustrade. In five minutes, she had recovered her beatific smile and dreamy stare. It was as if a fish had never even nibbled at the bait she had so meticulously set out.

Danny Moses, whom I'd also pumped for information on the sailfish, is a vociferous champion of angling as a Goan pastime. 'It's a social thing, but it's also a chance for us to spend some time alone with nature—that's why we do it,' he told me, when we first met at a coffee shop in Panaji. Moses has been fishing for as long as he can remember, and like nearly every one of his fellow Goans, he said, he has a favourite spot for fishing alone: near the jail just off Coco Beach. 'I like to fish as the tide goes out, and all the mullet come down, so the bigger fish like the bream and the barramundi all gather, waiting to eat.'

But in his lifetime—in less than half his lifetime, in fact—Moses has seen his average catch dwindle, even as Goa has tried to keep its climbing numbers of tourists sated with the seafood they desire. 'For seven years, this has been a fish-starved state. So much of the fish we buy now comes to us from Karnataka and Maharashtra,' he said. 'Ten years ago, in this very bay'— just opposite our chairs on Miramar Circle—'you could put in a net and just pull out the mullet. Today, you'll get nothing.' Moses twisted in his chair and pointed to a girl sitting with her friends on the opposite side of the café. 'You see her? Her dad was one of the first people to get a trawler, way back in the early 1980s. He got a whole fleet. Now he has only one boat, because the catch is that much poorer these days,' he said. 'People have to realize, within themselves, what they stand to lose. I don't want to even imagine a world where my son will not see a single salmon in the river. And it's all just a classic case of greed.'

Moses held up a hand and starting ticking off, on fleshy fingers, the items in this litany of greed; after Number Three, he abandoned the count and simply began karate-chopping the air in despair. He condemned the trawlers ripping up the seabed even in the two-kilometre zone from the coastline that is reserved by law for traditional fishing. He talked, through gritted teeth, about rules broken with impunity or tripped up by corruption, of surreptitious fishing even during the two-month closed season, about the pernicious stake nets, 'banned everywhere else in the world, but here they're put up even in the breeding areas of the river, so that all the fry are caught.' He dissected the perpetual state of confrontation between the trawler owners and the ramponkas, the traditional fishermen using the artisanal rampon nets. That conflict has been seething since the 1970s, but even today, he said, every year some boats are burned. 'This is an outright war.'

Moses was fond of tying this dystopian fishing culture to the larger loss of an older Goa—a Goa where, fifteen years ago, if somebody found a lost bag or wallet, they'd put an advertisement in the newspaper, and the money would all be there when it was claimed. There were no such advertisements in the newspapers any more, he said. The Goa of today hangs on exultantly to its lost bags and wallets; it is brasher and greedier and cockier, and often at odds with itself. 'Earlier, we'd go inland to fish, and you know, we'd catch one fish and have a good time and come away,' he said. I could almost see the roseate glaze on his eyeballs. 'Now, you see kids in these four-wheel drives camping out there, with loud music and bright lights, and they'll catch as many fish as they can. It's making the locals in these places really angry. If they catch you now, they'll break your rod and chase you away.'

These were largely the complaints, Moses acknowledged, of a hobbyist fisherman; the situation of the professional fishermen, he said, was far more dire. A couple of days earlier, I had met Claude Alvares, a fierce-looking environmentalist who has for years been railing against the damage that the tourism industry has wrought upon Goa's beaches and therefore the fishing trade. (His web site, not inaccurately, identifies him as a Typewriter Guerilla.) Alvares' office is in a hilly section of Mapusa, on the ground floor of an apartment building that also houses a grocery shop and a stationer's. He is a busy man, forever awash in appointments; he is also prone to forgetting about those appointments when he has built up a head of conversational steam, when his white moustache has begun to quiver with the indignation he feels.

Broken down into its smallest unit, according to Alvares, the problem was that of the Goan beach shack. Enjoyable as it can be, the culture of the beach shack is premised entirely on artificiality. The shack is an artificial way to be 'outdoors' on the public beach, where alcohol isn't allowed, and to still be 'indoors,' where turning down alcohol can constitute a grave breach of the Goan tourists' social code. It is an artificial way for tourists to feel like they're being hippies in authentic Goa and communing with the waves all day, even as they know that they will drive back to their air-conditioned hotel rooms for the night. Even the poverty-stricken label of 'shack' sits uneasily with the Rs 120 beers and the Rs 220 fish fry being served under its thatched roof. And as the final twist, that roof itself is only as permanent as the visitors it shelters. When a tourist season ends, the shacks are dismantled and put away as easily as if they were made of Lego bricks, to be broken out again only for the next season of beach-bumming and wave-communing. It is as if, out of tourist season, there were really no cafés in Rome.

'So all the time, in Goa, there is this pressure for more shacks on the beaches,' Alvares said. 'This year, for instance, there are three hundred shack licenses being given out by the government, and the funny thing is, this is despite a 25 per cent drop in the number of tourists. Next year, they'll give out four hundred licenses. Then there are the deck beds—as many as three thousand of them on Goa's beaches and more to come next year. The people in the government never have any brains, so there's never any limit to this nonsense.'

This contest between the tourism and fishing industries was really no contest at all. The creep of shacks has slowly edged the fishing canoes off the beaches, the jet-skis and power-boats have kept the coastal waters in constant churn and driven away the fish, and the beachfront developers have bought or grabbed all the land they could. 'There used to be twenty to twenty-five fishing boats at a time on Baga beach, but now there are barely a couple,' Alvares said. So the fishermen, deprived of the space to practise their profession, had to give it up and turn, in the blackest irony, towards the only viable source of employment: tourism. They bought shacks, or they opened water-sport businesses, or they joined the hotels. Thus, in Alvares' narrative of capitalism gone bad, the industry grew fatter still, forced more fishermen out of business, lured them into its folds and crevices, grew fatter still, and so forth.

'Then there's the sand,' Alvares went on. 'Go look at Anjuna beach—it is that weirdest of things, a sandless beach. They're carting away the sand dunes to put into the plinths of all these new buildings that are coming up. Studies say that by 2020, with a rise in the sea level, 5 to 10 per cent of Goa will go under. But still they're destroying these protective sand dunes.' He had written about some of this, he said, in his book *Fish Curry and Rice*, which aggressively identifies itself, in its subtitle, as *A Citizens' Report on the Goan Environment*. 'But funnily, nobody wants to read about these things in Goa, because nobody seems to care,' Alvares lamented. 'You'd probably have a better chance of finding that book in Mumbai or New Delhi.'

Alvares had two pieces of advice for me. The first was to stop talking to him, and to others like him, and to instead start visiting the beaches themselves, to talk to the fishermen I would meet. The second was to simply walk along the stretch of beach between Calangute and Candolim, to the rusting hulk of the *River Princess*, a ship that had run aground in north Goa in the June of 2000 and still remained in exactly the same place eight years later. Only then, Alvares said, would I be able to learn for myself the extent of the government's greed and inefficiency, and to see in process the destruction of the fisherman's habitat.

On the way out of Alvares' office, I stopped at the stationer's in the same building to ask for *Fish Curry and Rice*, but they didn't have it in stock. Over the next two days, I must have asked for the book in at least half a dozen bookstores across Goa. I didn't find a single copy.

Following Alvares' advice, I began my own variation on the beach-hopping itinerary that every tourist in Goa seems to follow, and for this I relied largely on the wisdom and street smarts of George Francis Borges. Borges is a short, pugnacious individual, so baby-faced that it came as a faintly obscene shock to learn that he was thirty-seven, and that he was married with children. When he was a young man, he left Goa to work in the Middle East, returning when the first Gulf War began. 'Then I was a boating instructor on and off, but mostly I just sat around drinking. The problem was, I had too many friends, you know?' he told me with a lopsided smile. 'Money would come into this hand, go out of this hand. That's how it was.' When I met him, Borges was professionally a doer of a little bit of this and some of that. He assisted his friends with their business if he felt like it, and if Bollywood's movie units came to Goa to shoot, he helped out in his capacity of local guide and gopher. When *Dhoom* filmed there, Borges mentioned, he would zip around town bearing John Abraham on the pillion of his motorcycle, ferrying him from location to location. 'But otherwise, I just hang around,' he said. 'I go fishing a couple of times a week, on a friend's boat. Here in Goa, even if you don't like to fish, you go fishing—just to pass the time.' On our way to the offices of the Mandovi Fishermen Marketing Co-Op Society on the Betim jetty, Borges pointed to a ramshackle, abandoned shed by the riverside, near Reis Magos. 'You see there? That's my favourite spot to fish in all Goa.'

Sitakant Kashinath Parab, the chairman of the Society and like everyone else in Goa, a friend of Borges, has eyes that are appropriately reminiscent of a fish, blank and unblinking. His brief does not so much include the hundred-odd kilometres of Goa's coastline as the two-hundred-and-fifty-odd kilometres of its river systems. On the subject of the beaches, therefore, he was vague; he ventured that perhaps 50 per cent of the coastal fishermen had moved into tourism, but he offered this suspiciously round statistic uncomfortably. When we started talking about the rivers, however, he began to give us his fullest attention, his eyes leaving the piles of papers on his government-green metal desk and only rarely thereafter flickering to odd spots on the room's ugly blue walls.

Parab was eager to blame the ongoing demise of fishing on what I had thought, until then, were unquestionably pillars of social progress. The improved highway system, for instance, now trucked fish into Goa from Tamil Nadu, Orissa and Gujarat, and Parab considered it competition that Goa's fishermen didn't need. Education had improved, but because of this 'literation,' Parab moaned, fishermen began to aim for sophisticated, white-collar jobs. 'It's not just fishermen, in fact,' Parab said. 'One of my friends comes from a family of toddy tappers, and in their village, there used to be a thousand people just tapping toddy. But in the next generation, there isn't a single person who knows how to climb a coconut tree. And my friend now owns a tourist boat.'

Then there are the trawlers. 'You know,' Parab told us, 'the government of Goa stopped issuing licenses for new trawlers some time ago. But they do still issue renovation licenses.' So instead of officially buying new trawlers, Goa's fishing magnates constantly 'renovate' their old vessels magically into trawlers with bigger holds and newer engines. 'What can we do? We can't even tell our fishermen to continue in this loss-making profession,' Parab said. 'And if a fisherman who earns Rs 100 a day can sell his land for Rs 10 lakhs, start a lease-a-motorbike service, make Rs 1,000 a day by renting out five motorcycles, and sit at home all day playing cards and drinking, who wouldn't do it? People are too idle, and that type of idle income is possible only in a tourist economy like Goa's.' Perhaps I was mistaken, but I thought I caught a wistful note in Parab's voice as he outlined that landscape of laziness.

I asked, at this point, about the riverboat casinos that I had seen in Panaji, and it was like setting off a depth charge in already choppy waters. 'Until a few years ago, there was only one riverboat casino—the *Caravela*,' Parab exploded. The *M. V. Caravela*, named after the first Portuguese armada to visit Goa in the sixteenth century, has been operating its Casino Goa since 2001. 'Now there are five more. Every night, each boat hosts between three and five hundred guests, in addition to a hundred-odd staff. So in one night, untreated waste from thousands of people, not to mention plastic and other litter, is released into the river.' Parab estimated that the Goan government received a Rs 1 crore license fee from each casino; in fact, a couple of months after I met him, the government increased that figure to Rs 5 crores. 'When that's the kind of money coming in,' Parab said, 'why would the government even listen to us?'

It isn't, he added, that the fishermen haven't tried. 'I've gone personally to the fisheries department to ask them why they were sitting idle'—that word again—'and why they weren't doing something to protect the fishing community.' But the department itself, Parab muttered darkly, had sold its soul—or to be more exact, had rented it out. 'They used to be on the ground floor and first floor of a building, with a jetty attached,' he said. But the department had given over the jetty as well as the ground floor offices to the owners of the *Caravela*. 'The fisheries department itself owns three trawlers, but now it has nowhere to park them,' Parab said. 'What will this kind of department do?'

From Betim, Borges took me to Coco Beach on the Mandovi estuary, which popular opinion regarded as the most degraded stretch of beach in Goa. There was, in reality, not much beach left. I saw Coco as a grubby bar of mud, covered with a thin film of sand that was only cosmetic in its presence, and overrun by a litter of nets and fishing paraphernalia. After hectic, unplanned development had weakened the soil, the beach had been eaten away by the sea and the monsoon rains. 'There would be shacks from there to there,' Borges indicated, his arm moving in a wide arc over the beach. As Coco got narrower, the shacks began to trespass onto a traditional fishing stronghold, and the fishermen protested loudly enough to, in a rare victory, have them shut down. But the damage had been done; Coco now looks like something the tourism monster has masticated and spat back out.

It was a hot day, and a group of fishermen was just launching a boat out to sea when we arrived, so we waited in the shade of a scraggly clump of trees for Reginald Silvera to finish issuing his instructions to them. Silvera, thirty years old, had been a fisherman at Coco Beach since he left school in the eighth grade to follow his father into the profession, catching mackerel, sardines, prawn and kingfish in the sea. His hair had the brittle, thirsty appearance that is bestowed by too much salty air, and his skin had been stained a dark walnut by the sun. In his immediate family, he was the only Silvera still fishing actively. 'I set up a shack on Calangute beach a few years ago, but my brother runs that. And my other brother has a tourist boat business,' he told me. 'But you know, with a shack, you have to be on the beach for twelve hours every day. Who wants to do that?' (I could think of a few people, I thought to myself.) 'Here, I can go fishing even at night, if I want to. Fishing is my life, and it's a good life. But not everybody feels that way. Many of my friends have drifted away into the tourism business.'

Silvera, like other Goan fishermen I would meet over the next few days, seemed to consider it a matter of pride and honour to insist that he had stayed true to his fishing roots, and that he had stopped his ears to the seductive call of the tourism business even as his colleagues succumbed to it. A further fillip of honour was to be derived from pointing out that, unless you are on a trawler, the fishing today is more difficult than ever. During a lull in our conversation, when Silvera went further down the beach to talk to another man, Borges advised me not to believe everything I heard. 'Many of these guys own their shacks on one side, have somebody else in the family run them, and fish only when they really feel like they want to,' he said. 'You just watch. He'll come back now and tell you about how hard it is to even get a decent catch of fish these days.'

Sure enough, Silvera returned and, as if he were picking up where he had left off, lunged with urgency into the subject of the 'hook long line' and the evil it had brought to Goan fishing. The hook long line, Borges had to explain to me later, is a rope of nylon that floats on the surface of the ocean, lashed to buoys at either end, and with thirty or more hooks suspended, by thinner lines, at intervals along the length of the rope. It is artisanal fishing's equivalent of the bulldozer, but it is deployed with the sweet, almost childlike hope of the ultimate bonanza—of pulling it up again with fish on every single hook, like a clothesline of stockings stuffed to capacity with Christmas presents.

The scourge of the hook long line, Silvera said, had hit Goan fishing hard. 'We Goan fishermen don't use it ourselves—it's used more by fishermen from outside the state, especially fishermen from the south of India,' he said. 'They bait a line with even a hundred hooks at a time, and it's very effective, especially with kingfish. But it catches fish of all ages, so between that and the trawlers, the waters are completely overfished. Earlier, our boats would go out, and every single boat would land a catch. Now, one day I may catch some fish, tomorrow you may catch some. Nothing is certain any more.'

A few hours later, on the road to Aguada, Borges spotted a man riding a coughing moped ahead of us, suddenly exclaimed: 'That's Alex!' and asked the driver to work the horn as he yelled out of the window for Alex to stop. (Borges did this often. We would be driving along, and suddenly he would whip open the window, stick his head out like a dog, and holler at people whom he thought he knew. On at least a couple of occasions, he received confused glances in response, but as he ducked back in, he philosophically shrugged off these cases of mistaken identity as one of the regrettable facts of life.) Alex reined in his miserable steed, parked it in the middle of his lane, and sauntered into our car for a chat. Around us, the traffic accommodated uncomplainingly, making do with half a road instead of one.

Borges introduced Alex de Souza to me as one of the few remaining fishermen who fished alone, purely for himself. He made it sound like the temperament of an eminent concert soloist who played for personal satisfaction, and Alex's perpetual grin widened slightly. He had cheap sunglasses pushed back over his hair, which had been bleached into a rust-brown by the elements and which he had gathered into a ponytail. He wore a psychedelic blue T-shirt, the slogan on which proclaimed that its owner had 'NO FEAR'. He was just on his way to Aguada, he drawled, to have a look at his boat. It was all he seemed to have on his agenda for the day.

When I met him, Alex owned a two-seater canoe, and it is unlikely that he has diversified his holdings since then. For some extra money, he occasionally drove his friend's tourist boat, but for a living, he rowed two kilometres out at 4 a.m. every day and fished for red snapper, flathead and the occasional lobster. 'I put the net out, take a nap for an hour or so, pull it up again, and then repeat the process,' he said. Towards the middle of the morning, he returned to shore, and his mother kept some of his catch and sold the remaining at the market. Alex was in his mid-thirties, and he had been leading this life for a couple of decades already.

'But as the older fishermen die off, there are fewer of us who continue to go out fishing,' Alex said. 'My friends have tended to drift off into tourism, and the younger kids never fished at all, they went straight into the water sports business.' His beloved beaches near Aguada have been ruined by the tourist trade as well. 'The shacks accumulate all this garbage, but instead of disposing of it, they dig these holes in the sand and bury them there,' he said. 'Then the monsoon comes and washes the sand away, and the garbage comes pouring back out.' Even if somebody did clear the trash, the pits remained, to be augmented during the next tourist season by more pits, the beach slowly transformed into a landscape of Swiss cheese.

On another day, we drove to the Sinquerim jetty, the shooting location, Borges informed me with his inside knowledge, of the famous *Dhoom* scene featuring a boat leaping over a bridge. The jetty pushes into a narrow channel of water, on either side of which lines of palm trees grant blessed shade from the sun. From this convenient point, Borges' friends Mickey and Dominic ran their boat rental service, along with half a dozen other water sport entrepreneurs. The jetty was thrumming with jet-skis and powerboats, and this was in the first week of October, when it was still too early for tourists; during the peak of the season, I thought, the channel must positively swarm with craft, scudding through like hordes of angry water beetles.

Both Mickey and Dominic come from fishing families in Candolim; Dominic, in fact, was the president of the North Goa Fishermen's Union, although he admitted that the title did more to mark him out as a member of a bureaucracy than to mark him out as a fisherman. 'We started in water sports full time two years ago, simply because the catch wasn't good,' Dominic said. For many years, Dominic's family had fished just off the Goan shore in canoes, catching mostly mackerel and sardines. But when motorboats became cheaper, so did the temptation to buy them and lease them out to tourists. 'At first, we were just taking the hippies out to see the dolphins,' he grinned. As the fishing withered, the tourist trade flourished; for Mickey and Dominic, the move from one to the other was inevitable. And they were, clearly, the more prosperous for it. Their shirt pockets bulged with compact, complex-looking cell phones and expensive sunglasses, and a large diamond stud gleamed like a sunburst against the dark skin of Mickey's left ear lobe. I recalled Parab's ethical dilemma—how to convince fishermen to continue fishing when it was probably in their best interests to do otherwise—and I did not envy him his duty of grappling with it.

Only on my final full day in Goa was I able to follow the second part of Alvares' advice: to walk the beach from Calangute to Candolim. I reached Calangute early in the evening, with an hour to go before the sun doused itself in the far waters to the west. It was Saturday, and I had expected a crowd, but Calangute was only comfortably populated, mostly by Goans enjoying a rare chance to have their beach to themselves. A couple of loud cricket games were in progress, sending tennis balls scooting across the sand like fluorescent yellow crabs. Fathers in rolled-up trousers introduced their children to the ocean. At one spot, two shirtless men stood holding one end of a yellow line that ran away into the water, waiting patiently for a bite.

Even from Calangute, the bulk of the *River Princess* is clearly visible on the horizon, looking like a gigantic beached whale. She is something of an optical illusion, making for such a massive object for the eye to focus on that she dupes the mind into believing that the walk is shorter than it really is. Inexplicably left in her place for nearly a decade, the *River Princess* had settled, I later read, eight to ten metres into the seabed and had taken on more than thirty thousand metric tonnes of sand; moving her now, a salvage expert had proclaimed in the media, would be 'like uprooting a sunken four-storeyed building.' The briny air had chewed her eight-hundred-foot-long superstructure into streaks of rust and black, and claws of corroded steel regularly broke away into the water or washed up onto the shore.

When she was still alive, the *River Princess* was an ore-carrier belonging to Salgaocar Mining Industries, but after she expired one rainy night on a sandbar off Candolim, her owner was able to abandon the corpse without inviting penal action of any kind. When the wreck became a blight on a popular beach, Goans reasonably expected the state to tow her away, if only out of a self-interested desire to protect the tourist trade, its golden goose. Instead, the *River Princess* now began to be mired in the far swampier waters of bureaucracy. A lawsuit ineffectually travelled to the Goa bench of the Mumbai High Court; a 2001 act to protect tourist spots in Goa, designed and passed specifically for the removal of the *River Princess*, did nothing; multiple governments issued multiple salvage tenders that went nowhere. Meanwhile, the *River Princess* sank further into her grave, altering the tidal flow around her, peeling into the sea. From a distance, she resembled a jagged dagger stabbed into Goa's soft curves.

Walking towards the ship, I passed lines of beach eateries, boarded up for the off-season. More shacks would soon be assembled along the route I was taking, and I could see the tracks of their former passage—the small, shallow garbage-pits that Alex had mentioned. To my left, there were deep gouges in a higher level of sand, so regular that they were clearly artificial;

some of them were broad and semi-circular, and when they occurred one after another, it looked as if a giant mouth had taken a clean bite out of the coast. The beach had little sand to spare; the ground felt hard under my feet, not as if the sand had been packed by water but as if there was brick or clay just beneath.

It took me thirty minutes to come near enough to the *River Princess* to be able to spot the irregular gashes above her waterline and the individual flakes of peeling paint on her skin. Surprisingly—or, in the light of everything else associated with this mess, perhaps not so surprisingly—there were no signs posted to urge people not to go wading or swimming near the wreck. The wind swept in and out of her hull with forlorn whistles. At such close quarters, the *River Princess* stopped being an eyesore, because it was easier to see her for what she was: An honest vessel, left to desolation and decay through no fault of her own. Alvares had called the *River Princess* a symbol of the inefficiency of Goa, but that didn't feel quite right. She was more a symbol of the indolence of Goa, of a state that had come to be unfortunately infected with the idleness of its guests.

8
On seeking to eat as a city once ate

Every minute of the half hour I waited for Yashwant Chimbaikar outside his house, I worried that he simply wouldn't turn up. When I had met him for the first time a few days earlier, at 7.30 in the evening, he was already tipsy, and I worried that he wouldn't remember our appointment or even remember me. I worried that the wedding he had attended the previous night, from which he'd reportedly returned at 2 a.m., had proven to be such a fount of liquor that he wouldn't stir for the rest of the day, and certainly not at half past five on a chilly Mumbai morning. I worried at the prospect of banging on what I uncertainly suspected was his door, and thereby rousing an entire extended family—possibly the wrong extended family. So I just stood and shivered and repeatedly did what he had asked me to do: Call his mobile phone.

Chimbaikar, a fish vendor, lives in Chimbai, one of the many Koli settlements within Mumbai; traditionally, these were discrete villages, but as a city grew up in the gaps around them, they might now be called, less charitably, ghettoes. Chimbai's Kolis,

Chimbaikar among them, are largely fisher folk, either fishermen or fish sellers. Every morning, just before dawn, little posses of Chimbai residents leave in two or three trucks for Mumbai's docks, returning around half past nine with great quantities of fresh fish, to be sold through the remainder of the day. That trip to the docks was ordinarily the preserve of Narmada, Chimbaikar's wife, but Yeshi (as he insisted I call him) was making an exception for me. 'Come by at 5.30 on Saturday morning and we'll go to the docks together,' he had said. 'Stand outside the Hotel Usha and just call this number. I'll come right out.'

Eventually, just before six, Yeshi did emerge, having apparently taken the extra minutes to look good for me. His thin grey hair was slicked neatly into place, and he wore a spotless white shirt, steel-coloured polyester trousers and a large pair of dark glasses with the brand 'Planet' inscribed on them. From his neck hung a gold chain with two pendants, one shaped like an anchor and the other like a ship's wheel. He could easily have passed for the captain of a private yacht on the Riviera. 'Did you wait long?' he asked. Without waiting for my answer, he headed towards a small shrine for a prayer—the village of Chimbai is half Christian and half Hindu—and then into the Hotel Usha for a glass of tea. 'Come, sit, there's no hurry,' Yeshi said. 'Besides, I really need the tea.'

Even at that time of the day, the No. 1 bus from Chimbai to south Mumbai was surprisingly full. We passed Mumbai in various stages of the act of waking up—still lolling in bed half-asleep at Mahim, sitting up and rubbing its eyes on a flyover near Byculla, and heading out for a jog at the already active Chor Bazaar. 'If your car is ever stolen,' Yeshi said, as we passed the Bazaar, 'within an hour, it will have been brought here and stripped for parts.'

Yeshi is, in general, a fund of information about all sorts of

Mumbai commerce. Once, he told me about how lemons were sold at the wholesale market. 'No words are involved, nobody says anything. The guy puts his hand in your shirt and holds up some fingers,' he said, and by way of immediate demonstration, he stuck his clammy, rough hand up my shirt and raised a finger and a thumb. 'You touch that hand, feel the bid, and respond. The bargaining goes on like this, all blind, so that nobody else can see the prices you're getting.'

When the No. 1 bus let us off near Sassoon Docks, Yeshi became even more authoritative; the Docks, after all, had been a part of his life for nearly every one of his sixty years. 'The guard at the gate there, you see him? He gets a bribe of Rs 50 per truck, otherwise he won't let it leave the Docks,' he said. 'Each cop here makes at least Rs 2,000 every day as bribes. You see that man, walking away from us, dressed in white? He's one of the six local dons.' Then, with unalloyed glee at the prospect, Yeshi added: 'Each one of those dons has six or seven women all to himself.'

The Sassoon Docks was completed in 1875, when its eponymous builder Albert Abdullah David Sassoon had already been made a knight, and when baronetcy lay a few years into the future. The first 'wet dock' in western India, Sassoon Docks was built over three years on 200,000 square feet of land mostly wrested back from the sea, with an uninterrupted view of a bumpy little island called Oyster Rock. Over the years, it has come to be dominated almost exclusively by the fishing trade, therefore serving, every morning, simultaneously as a wharf and a marketplace. When I visited, it was one of the few docks still open to visitors, but a withered paper notice pasted near the entrance warned that, very soon, only people with entry permits would be allowed in.

Through a pair of large metal gates, past a double row of stalls selling frail plastic watches, monkey caps, flowers and breakfast, was a long concrete platform that extended into the ocean, packed with docked fishing boats on either side. Part of that stretch was roofed, so that it resembled a large open shed, virtually every square inch of it agitating with activity. Koli fisherwomen sat and argued over prices, or they walked purposefully about, cane baskets on their heads, elbowing aside whatever stood in their way. Spot auctions progressed in a sign language that Yeshi had to explain to me. ('Put your little finger up, and you're raising the bid by Rs 100. Then every subsequent finger raised is another Rs 100, or you can put up half a finger for Rs 50. Put up all five fingers at once and you've raised the bid by Rs 1,000.') In the odd static clumps, little girls sat meditatively deveining prawns with nimble fingers.

Writers are fond of detecting rhythms of movement in even the most crowded, frenetic places—a reflection of the very writerly desire to impose order upon the disorder around them. At Sassoon Docks that morning, however, it was full-blown chaos. The only rhythm I could spot was a sort of reverse Brownian motion, particles of humanity rushing to avoid each other, people ducking and weaving out of each other's way, sidestepping and feinting and jostling and second-guessing. It was a waltz of discomfiture, a dance with a narrative that

Sassoon Docks teems with early-morning commerce

sought valiantly to preserve even a minimal bubble of personal space—a dance, really, choreographed across all of Mumbai, nearly all the time.

Yeshi seemed to know, even with a glance, exactly where every lot of fish was headed. 'That octopus will be exported to China,' he'd say, or, 'That tuna is going to be tinned. You know all the tinned tuna that's sold here in Mumbai as "Made in Japan"? Well, it isn't. It's tinned right here in Mumbai.' He stepped nonchalantly over long, thick tentacles that crept out of their cane baskets and straggled across the floor, as if they were about to engage in a climactic piece of dirty business in a horror movie. I didn't even recognize some of the truly odd-shaped monsters; one, I could have sworn, was a whole hammerhead shark, but with a wonky nose, dumped casually on a scrap of torn blue tarpaulin.

As the day brightened further, Yeshi walked me up and down the waterfront, past the ice machines and the groups of fishermen playing cards and the Indian Oil Corporation trucks. His arm draped fraternally about my shoulder, he had moved on from talking about fish to imparting well-meaning lessons on life. 'I had a cousin, older to me, who was greedy—always after money, looking for ways to get richer,' he said, for instance. 'He died at the age of forty-five.' Then, a few steps further, another moral: 'My own father lived to be a hundred and five. He told us, his five sons, to never be fearful. If you are, you'll die of fear before you accomplish anything.'

In 1959, when Yeshi was twelve years old, his mother died, and he left school in the seventh grade to start working on boats for 50 paise a day. In his community, and for his generation, that was still an unusually rich education. 'The other fishermen still come to me to figure out their expenses. I used to like arithmetic in school,' he said. Then, as if reluctant to divulge one fond boyhood memory without another, he said: 'You know, I met

Jawaharlal Nehru when he came to our school. I even shook his hand.'

For twelve years, from 1969 to 1981, Yeshi was a member of the Shiv Sena, Bal Thackeray's political party that dedicated itself to aggressive Marathi chauvinism. 'But then I quit,' Yeshi said. 'They filled their stomachs while our blood flowed. We got nothing out of it.' He seemed to regard that period of his life with the slightly disbelieving amusement of an old man considering the follies of his heady youth. So what did he think, I asked him, of the events of the last few days—of Bal Thackeray's nephew Raj and his Maharashtra Navnirman Sena's campaign to guard Marathi identity, of its violence against north Indian immigrants who allegedly spirited away the jobs of 'genuine' Mumbaikars from right under their noses?

'Look, where are you from?' Yeshi asked.

'Madras,' I said.

'Right. So say you come here from Madras. And you work hard, you work wholeheartedly,' he postulated. 'I'm from Mumbai. Now, if I don't work as hard, why should you be blamed?' It was really as simple as that, Yeshi said, and he smiled, this man from the most ancient, most authentic community of Mumbaikars.

The Kolis, Salman Rushdie rightly pointed out in *Midnight's Children*, were here first, 'when Bombay was a dumbbell-shaped island, tapering at the centre to a narrow shining strand beyond which could be seen the finest and largest natural harbour in Asia.' They were, almost overwhelmingly, fisher folk, and the very word 'koli' translates to both 'spider' and 'fisherman' because, as the historian D.D. Kosambi once explained, the fisherman uses his net much as a spider uses its web. Even as modern Mumbai marginalized her eldest children, pushing them into their ever-tighter villages, the Kolis left their stamp on the city in nomenclature: their Kolibhat became today's Colaba, their Palva Bunder became today's Apollo Bunder, and their goddess Mumbadevi became today's Mumbai.

I had come to Mumbai in search of some of these original Mumbaikars, and as if he were doing me a perverse sort of favour, Raj Thackeray began his agitations the day before I arrived, raising again in people's minds that old question: Who exactly is the original Mumbaikar? It could be the Koli, but it could just as well be any of the members of subsequent waves of migration into the city from Gujarat, Goa or South India—or from Bihar and Uttar Pradesh, the migrant workers who were bearing the undeserved brunt of this particular cycle of Thackeray's viciousness. When their leader was arrested, the members of the MNS took to stopping taxis on roads and, if their drivers were found to be from North India, beating them and torching their vehicles. 'There is lafda everywhere,' I was warned, that wonderful Mumbai slang word for trouble suggesting nothing as much as an inordinate crease or tear in the space–time continuum.

As a result, at the normally traffic-choked time of 7.30 p.m. on my first day there, the roads were so bereft of taxis and other cars that it might have been 3.30 a.m. When I took a taxi home, my driver entered into hectic consultations with his fellow cabbies about the safest possible route. Then, throughout the journey, his eyes flickered constantly to the sides of the road, alert for any imminent danger. Suddenly every man who held up his hand to cross the road, a regular enough practice on any other day, had to be viewed with circumspection, and it was actually a relief when once we ran into a jammed intersection. 'You know, I wasn't even sure about taking you,' my driver said as I was paying him at the end of the jittery ride. 'Anybody could be trouble at such a time. Absolutely anybody.'

Thackeray had been arrested in the late afternoon, when I was at the Mumbadevi Temple in the heart of Zaveri Bazaar, a busy labyrinth of commerce that perfectly symbolized the city to which the goddess had given her name. Even one of the entrances into the Temple's complex has been pinched almost into non-existence by the shops to either side of it. 'Without all this Raj Thackeray lafda, we'd have a lot more people here by now,' a security guard said as he waved me through a beeping, utterly useless metal detector. 'You'd have had a difficult time even squeezing through.'

Climbing the few steps up into the temple—each rendered permanently sticky underfoot by the spilled juice of hundreds of smashed coconuts—I entered a small sanctum with two individual shrines. One, containing a moon-faced idol of Annapurna flanked by two heavily mustached bronze soldiers, seemed forlorn and ignored; instead, the crowds congregated in little clumps around the other shrine, bearing a low statue of Mumbadevi, a fierce-looking, orange goddess with ten arms. The idol was more face than body: It was easier to spot, for instance, the large ornament in her left nostril than the diminutive lion she rode. Long stalks of purple and pink flowers fanned out behind her, and she wore a classic Maharashtrian green saree, which was constantly being adjusted this way or that by the bored priest sitting alongside her.

On the silvered doors of the shrine, the Koli legend of Mumbadevi has been etched in simple panels. There once lived, in these parts, a powerful giant named Mumbarak, who wangled from Brahma the boon that he would never meet his death at another's hands. Unsurprisingly, this power went to Mumbarak's head, and when he began to throw his considerable weight about as indestructible giants will do, the gods sought the protection of the other two members of the trinity, Vishnu and Shiva. Out of their combined power, a lion-riding Devi was born, and in a

Following Fish

fight that must have lasted many exciting rounds, she beat Mumbarak to within an inch of his life. Then, in an act of grace, she granted Mumbarak a final blessing: that his name should be joined with hers, to be perpetuated on Earth. The city of Mumbai, it would appear, is the fulfillment of that dying wish.

Mumbadevi may have begun as a Koli goddess, but she became, long ago, the patron deity of her entire city. Mumbaikars across communities, castes and languages visit her temple; when I was there, I heard Marathi and Hindi, but also Malayalam, Punjabi and Gujarati. Mothers brought their babies in to be blessed. Businessmen prayed for their businesses in between cell phone calls. Students with a month to go for their final exams looked to Mumbadevi for divine inspiration. A trio of grandfathers sat in front of the shrine, their lips fluttering in silent prayer.

Squatting on the floor, taking notes, I was approached by a boy who must have been five or six years old, offering me a crumbling lump of peda in his open palm. I broke off a little for myself. Then he looked curiously at my notebook and asked: 'What are you writing? Are you doing your homework?'

'Yes,' I said. I wasn't at home, but apart from that, it was a pretty good approximation.

'Homework!' he said, made a face of utter disgust, and ran away. Meanwhile, behind me, his mother continued to pray that her son would work hard and excel at his studies.

☙

Of the many migrant communities who gravitated to Mumbai and who, over decades, began to regard themselves as 'authentic Mumbaikars,' the mill-workers of the nineteenth century are among the most prominent. The first cotton mill opened in Bombay in 1851, and demand jumped in the 1860s, when Great Britain found its access to cotton from the American south cut off by port blockades during the American Civil War. The workers driving Bombay's mills were largely from the city's hinterland, particularly the Konkan districts of Ratnagiri and Sindhudurg, where agriculture was often disrupted by floods or excess rain. According to one estimate, there were over 100,000 mill workers in the city by 1892, living in the cramped tenements that we know as chawls. Most were men, who having left their wives and families behind in their villages, had to find a way to feed themselves.

This would turn out to be the genesis of a network of 'lunch homes' or 'khanawals,' Mumbai's variant of the unfussy working-class canteens that exist, in one form or another, in every city in India. In a book called *Dharma's Daughters*, Sara S. Mitter describes how the chawls' residents had little facility or energy to cook, and they were certainly too impecunious to eat at regular restaurants. So housewives began to offer daily board to small batches of mill workers, covering their own family's food expenses in the process; the mill workers would pay for their meals at the end of the month, when they got their wages. The lunch home was a hard-nosed, businesslike affair: You came in purely to eat your stolid way through a plate of food, not to socialise or dawdle over your meal. But the food was good and cheap, and as Mitter writes, it tasted of home, which helped ease 'the anomie of a workingman's existence.'

One of Mumbai's best remaining khanawals, I was told, is Anantashram, which I located with considerable difficulty in the madness of Girgaum, in a small lane named Khotachiwadi. Like the other houses around it, Anantashram is an old wooden structure, and only one round signboard announces its presence. Next door is the Girgaum Catholic Club ('Members Only'), and just opposite is a little roadside chapel. When I finally found Khotachiwadi, squarely in the middle of lunchtime, the only signs of life were two men playing cards in the back seat of a dusty, lifeless Premier Padmini, and the constant ebb and flow of Anantashram's patrons.

Anantashram must be close to a century old, although it is difficult to ascertain this with any exactitude when its employees wear their antipathy to questions—and to photos, and really to anything that is not a single-minded pursuit of lunch—almost as a part of their uniforms. The waiters spoke only in extreme emergencies, and the customers—all men, when I went there— followed that lead. The dishes of the day were chalked up in Marathi on a blackboard; one waiter took one look at me and loosened his lips long enough to tell me that the English version, hanging in a back room, was severely outdated. Just inside the entrance—under portraits of Hanuman, Radha and Krishna, and an old gentleman who presumably founded Anantashram— sat the manager behind a high table. As each customer entered, the manager would utter one word—'Bangda'—and clam up again. But that was sufficient to deliver the message: The fish of the day was mackerel. In the kitchen at the back, a thin, sweating man in a vest and shorts wrestled with a long pair of tongs, flipping rotis on a griddle in the midst of so many open fires and bubbling pots that the scene looked positively infernal.

From the gloom, a waiter materialized and first brought me water in a squat, broad steel bowl, then a cool glass of the spiced kokum-coconut milk drink known as sol kadhi, and then a superb set lunch that sang of home: Rice, fresh rotis, an elongated piece of fried fish, a bowl of curry, and a piece of curried fish. The curried fish, perched on the rim of a bowl, seemed oddly aloof from its curry, as if they were an arguing couple arriving together at a party, for the sake of appearances, but determined to go their separate ways as soon as possible. The fry, hidden under the slim sheaf of rotis, was so tender that it was falling apart even as I picked it up, splitting down the middle to show off its beautiful palette: golden brown on the surface, green around the edges where the skin showed through, and a veneer of silver under the batter, like foil on a barfi.

For the entirety of my meal, though, it was the curry that held my attention. It was, more than anything else, a thick fish soup, flavoured heartily with mackerel, smooth with coconut, yellow with turmeric, tart with kokum, and finished with a flourish of tempered mustard seeds. I asked for a second helping of the curry, to go with the perfectly cylindrical serving of rice; of the curried mackerel itself, though, I was not a fan. It seemed to have given its all to its gravy, and it now sat glistening but essence-less on the edge of my plate. When I rose after my meal, in fact, that remaining hunk of fish earned me a scolding from my waiter for not finishing my food.

Like the old khanawals, Anantashram aimed to be strictly dedicated to the act of feeding. Lunch ended not at a fixed time but when the kitchen ran out of food, and many customers sat on a bench facing the wall, ate without a flicker of expression, and left within a quarter of an hour. But some informality sporadically weakened this rigour. The regulars seemed to know each other well, and conversation was sometimes sustained for three or four minutes on end. One surreal exchange, in particular, proved so diverting that I forgot all about my bangda curry for its duration, so that I could watch and listen with my fullest concentration.

A middle-aged man in jeans and a T-shirt, with a pony tail sprouting like an exotic plant out of the back of his head, came in, nodded to a gray-bearded Sikh in a baseball cap, and took a seat beside him. He ordered. A few minutes later, his food arrived, and he began to eat. After a few bites, he turned to his neighbour.

Pony Tail: So how's it going?

Baseball Cap: Okay, okay.

Pony Tail: In some time, anyway, we will all be naked.

This thought gave Baseball Cap considerable pause. Quite

possibly, he was not a long-term planner; perhaps he had only scheduled his day till lunch, or till the subsequent, honest post-lunch nap. Either way, it appeared that nudity had not really figured in his vision for the near future.

Baseball Cap: What?

Pony Tail, a little elliptically: Ya, it will be that hot in a couple of months, we'll want to just be naked. Because it got so cold this winter. So the other extreme will also happen.

Baseball Cap, considerably relieved: Ah.

Pony Tail: I've never worn warm clothes in Bombay. But I had to this time.

Baseball Cap: Anyway, the cold is over now.

Pony Tail: Yes.

Baseball Cap: Did you try the bangda? It's good.

Pony Tail: Mmmmm.

Baseball Cap: Bangda is healthy for you. Good for vitamins.

A spell of contented eating followed. There was to be no nudity after all.

In Mumbai, there can be considerable confusion about the precise school of cuisine to which Anantashram adheres. A quick poll revealed it to be decidedly Gomantak, although some also pointed out that popular misconception often held it to be Malvani. Both culinary influences reached Mumbai from regions to its south, further down India's western coast; both started to dig their roots in when migrants from those regions began to arrive in large numbers in the middle of the nineteenth century. But there are certainly tangible differences, and happily, I was told that the best way to figure those out would simply be to eat my way around Mumbai over the next few days.

So I did. I ate plates and plates of thin, fried bombil, or Bombay Duck; of chewy, salty mori, or baby shark; of mackerel fried, stuffed, curried or, one deeply unfortunate time, just boiled; of shrimp prepared in a manner that would simply be described as 'masala.' I drank many jugs of sol kadhi. I puttered, in taxis or on foot, through the congested lanes of Dadar and Mahim, my eyes restlessly searching for signboards bearing either of the two magic words, 'Gomantak' or 'Malvani.'

At Sushegad Gomantak, a small eatery opposite the Paradise Cinema in Mahim, I received a culinary master course from its rotund, middle-aged proprietress, who bridled at the suggestion that her food could often be confused for Malvani. 'They're completely different,' she snapped, and leaving her position behind the till, she joined me at my table, called over a waiter, and rattled off a chain of instructions in Marathi. He left us for five minutes, and returned with a tray of little dishes. Then he retreated to the rear of the room, to watch the proceedings with a waggle-toothed, smart-aleck grin on his face.

'First, eat some of that,' she said, pointing to a shallow saucer holding a few pieces of black, slightly desiccated kokum. Eaten raw, it had the sharp tang of citrus, and it left a lingering bitter aftertaste, not to mention fingers and teeth stained so thoroughly that they appeared to have been dyed in ink. 'The taste of kokum cuts through even the smoothest coconut-based curry,' my host said. 'Now, we use far less kokum in our masalas and curries than Malvani cooks do.' She paused for a second, considered that statement, and amended: 'Except in our sol kadhi.' Then she yelled back into the kitchen: 'Bring me some sol kadhi.'

For a beverage that is intended to act as a digestive and go easy on the stomach, sol kadhi has a complex cross-section of tastes. Drinking Sushegad Gomantak's sublime sol kadhi, coloured a pretty litmus purple by the kokum, I first tasted the coolness—if coolness can even be a taste—of its coconut milk, then the citrus of the kokum, then an intense riot of spices ('Pepper, mint, ginger, garlic, cloves and cumin. We spice our sol kadhi much more than Malvanis.'), and then, like an ingenious reprise, the coconut milk again, but this time for a final note of sweetness. I could, I think, have sat there all day drinking sol kadhi, but my instructor had further plans.

'Our curry,' she said, pushing a dish of mackerel gravy towards me, 'is heavier on the coconut, and less spicy. The Malvani curries will look and taste fierier.' Then she indicated another saucer containing a couple of small, dark seed pods. 'One thing we do have in common is that we both use split triphala in our curries.' I picked a pod up, turned it over with my fingers, and exactly one second before she remarked that it was best not to eat it raw, I popped it into my mouth.

This triphala was the product of a single plant, but there is also a synonymous Ayurvedic formulation of three distinct fruits (hence 'tri-phala') that is widely acclaimed for its medical benefits. When I was six or seven years old, my eyesight weakening from reading too much in poor light and my first pair of spectacles looking inevitable, my father procured a bottle of solution of the Ayurvedic triphala, having been told that it was good for the eyes. So, every morning for a few months, he would pour out some of the solution into a dark blue, eye-shaped cup, and I would sit at our dining table bathing each eye alternately. It was essential that I kept my eyes open as they marinated, and so, battling my blink reflexes, I would stare sightlessly into the stinging depths. When I emerged, I remember, I could feel each eyeball burning right around its circumference, but I persuaded myself that it was just the triphala at work. (It wasn't. I've been wearing glasses ever since.)

I mention this now because, very coincidentally, what that triphala did to my eyes, this triphala did to my tongue. After what felt like a miniature explosion set off inside my mouth, every individual taste bud began to quiver furiously, as if it were trying to shake itself loose of my tongue and escape into the recesses of my throat. It wasn't the tingling that comes with the heat of pepper; instead, this weird electricity rendered my tongue entirely numb to any other sensation. I drank two glasses of water and two shots of sol kadhi. Then I ate a couple of the fried pellets of shark, which I had found far too salty only minutes ago. It was no use: At least an hour passed before I was able to taste anything else.

The chatelaine of Sushegad Gomantak had placidly continued to hold forth during this traumatic period. 'You can think of Gomantak food in terms of the Goan influence, whereas Malvani food is specific to the region around Malvan, in the Sindhudurg district,' she appeared to be saying through the haze. 'That's a huge difference, whatever people may think.'

So did she like Malvani food?

'I wouldn't know,' she said with a tight smile. 'I've never had any.'

Only a few months later did I manage to make it to Malvan itself, driving for five hours from Goa into Maharashtra, and then following a pockmarked, gradually narrowing road into the small town—all just to eat lunch, wander around, and then eat an early dinner before driving back to Goa. I found a restaurant named, rather redundantly, Malvani, and decoding my old scribbled notes as I ate, I saw that my hostess had been perfectly right. Her sparse personal acquaintance with Malvani food notwithstanding, everything matched. The sol kadhi was paler, with less kokum but more pepper and ginger; the curry was ruddier and oilier, and its snarling heat was practically a declaration of war; the fried shark and fish had been rolled rapidly in pepper before they hit the oil. Beneath all that, of course, it was still the nobly pungent mackerel or bombil, humouring the minor, inter-regional tiffs of its supporting players like a truly magnanimous star performer.

Yeshi had told me, shortly before he fell asleep during our bus ride back from Sassoon Docks, that I would have a hard time finding an authentic Koli restaurant, and he was right. The Koli restaurant is a considerably rarer animal than the Gomantak or the Malvani restaurant, and the ubiquitous Prawn Koliwada and Chicken Koliwada are known to be utter fakes. The only way to eat Koli food, it appeared, was to shamelessly abuse somebody's hospitality and invite oneself over at mealtimes. That was how I met Gobind Patil.

Patil, a spry, white-haired man touching eighty, is the local leader of the 9,000-odd Kolis living in Danda Khar, very close to the sea. His father, in 1935, became the first practising advocate from the Koli community; his grandfather, also named Gobind Patil, was an ardent freedom-fighter, and he gave the Bandra municipality the land to build the main road that still bears his name. Patil lives in the ancestral house, more than 200 years old, with a high raftered ceiling and a massive central room, various parts of which have been designated to serve as living room, dining room and bedroom. 'Sixty years ago, you could look out of this window and see paddy fields and the sea,' Patil said, in his scratchy, wheezy voice. When I looked out of the window, I saw row upon row of pinched tenements, lives piled upon lives, a community collapsed upon itself like a dying star.

Patil has been cooking since he was in school, and cooking so well that his three daughters keep pressing him to write his recipes down. 'In primary school, after lunch, my two sisters and I would steal into the kitchen to make ourselves sirah, a type of kheer with milk and ghee and saffron,' Patil said. 'But what will I write down, you know? So many times, I change the ingredients of a dish at the very last moment, on intuition, and it always works. You can't write down that kind of thing.' Then an attack of acute shyness seized him, and he murmured almost to himself: 'The lunch we're eating today? I cooked it.'

In never becoming a professional chef, Patil had clearly missed his calling. At lunch, there was a ruddy kheema with plump prawns, a tuna curry, fried black pomfret, a side of greens that he cheerfully urged me to ignore, and paper-thin rotis made of rice-flour instead of wheat. The balance was exquisite: Less coconut and kokum than Gomantak or Malvani food, the pomfret fried in just a dusting of salt and spice, the curries subtle but not entirely without heat. 'The kheema is usually green, just made of ginger, coriander, green chillies, and garlic. But we weren't sure if you could take something that raw, so I made it with tomatoes and onions,' Patil told me with a wicked smile. Then he segued smoothly into a culinary gripe: 'So many Kolis today have stopped making their classic thick, green curry. Too many gravies are made of onion and tomato and curd. That's not the way it should be done.'

On topics related to food, Patil was a ready conversationalist; on topics unrelated, he would somehow reorient the compass of the discussion back towards food. Nearly everything we talked about seemed to remind him of a prawn masala he had once eaten, or air-dried, 'half-fresh' fillets of bombil fluttering on a line like strange flags in the winter breeze, or what Mumbai's mackerel used to taste like in the good old days. Once, I asked him about Koli fishermen, and about their fishing techniques. 'They're so lucky,' he sighed. 'They take pre-cooked rice and gravy out to sea on their boats, and when they catch fish, they just pop a couple into that gravy, and cook and eat them right there. They get the freshest catch of all.' I never found out anything from him about Koli fishing techniques.

About fish, Patil became particularly lyrical and expansive. 'It's so important to us that we sometimes even grind prawns or tuna or eel into our chicken or mutton masalas.' When he talked about the boiled fish, bland and easy to digest, that constitutes the first mouthful of solid food for many Koli children, he grew so sentimental and nostalgic that I had to wait a few minutes for him to break out of his Proustian moment. When he narrated the quiet, elemental joys of ukkad, a dish of very fresh pomfret boiled with salt and turmeric, he made it sound like a parable of the virtues of a simple life. When he described the Kolis' annual pilgrimages to Varanasi, during the monsoon, he dwelled with near-spiritual fervour on the dried Bombay Duck they would take along for the journey. When, en passant, the subject of the traditional Koli mud stove came up, he grabbed a wedding invitation lying on the table and proceeded to sketch in detail its circular cooking chamber and long flue. When he mentioned a dish called nisot, prepared often for the ailing, Patil halted himself abruptly, said, 'Nisot. We must have nisot now,' and over my feeble protests of not wanting to be any more trouble than I had already been, he dispatched his daughter Pravara into the kitchen to whip some up.

The unimaginative or the technically inclined would, I suppose, describe nisot as just a watery fish stock, but so much is lost in that translation. Nisot is the Koli challenge to chicken soup, a hearty brown broth perked up by a ground mixture of tamarind, small onions, chillies, coriander and garlic, in which a succulent mackerel or Bombay Duck has been boiled vigorously. The mackerel in Pravara's nisot had been cooked so thoroughly that it disintegrated into creamy flakes at the merest touch. Even the heady scent of that steamy broth—aromatic from the spices, piquant from the tamarind, and full of a wonderful, fishy infusion—should be sufficient to raise men from their deathbeds, let alone their sickbeds. On the invalid's tongue, the strong flavour of nisot must dance like champagne bubbles, homing in on the sinuses and restoring life to taste buds dulled by medication. It is nothing less than an elixir, the sort that seems worthy of being decanted into little round gourds, to be worn on the waists of fantasy-novel adventurers setting off for unknown lands.

After lunch, Patil pulled his ritual bottle of VAT 69 whisky towards him, offered me a glass, and poured himself three fingers' worth. 'I wish I could offer you some of our country liquor,' he said. 'It's made of dates and jaggery, and it tastes terrific.' The Kolis always drank a lot, he added, 'because the fishermen would find themselves working in both extremes of weather, hot or cold.' When he was in school, Patil told me, his father would host parties every Sunday, hosting luminaries like the Marathi author Prahlad Kesha 'Acharya' Atre. At the end of each such evening, Patil would nip downstairs, pour the leftover liquor from half a dozen bottles into a single glass, and drink that revolting cocktail neat.

Eventually, as afternoon slumped into evening, I asked Patil the question I had been asking everybody on this trip: What did he think of Raj Thackeray's chauvinistic formulas? It was the first time, and the only time, that I heard something different. 'I agree with him entirely,' Patil said. 'If people came to your city, Madras, and took away all your jobs, what would you do?' North Indians, he added, had even stirred up the fishing trade, buying fish wholesale and then undercutting the prices of Koli vendors. 'They've captured so much of our business. How, then, can we disagree with Thackeray?'

Patil told me that his father, Krishna Motiram Patil, was a member of the Rashtriya Swayamsevak Sangh, but that he was respected more for his knowledge of Hindu philosophy than for his position as a Hindu leader. 'My grandfather made bombs to use against the British,' Patil said. Once, family lore has it, when the police came around raiding the neighbourhood, his grandfather was on the top floor of the very house where his grandson lives today. 'Panicking, he packed up all the bomb material and hurled it into the sea from his window.' In case it was still unclear, Patil explained that this grandfather did not believe in ahimsa, Mahatma Gandhi's non-violent path that was captivating the imaginations of so many other Indians at the time. '"Ahimsa? What ahimsa?" my grandfather would say,' Patil remembered. '"If they attack you, you attack them."'

All right, I said, so perhaps he agreed with Thackeray's principles. But did he also agree with his methods?

To that question, I never got an answer. Patil had worked through most of his third glass of whisky, and he seemed content to just sit on his chair by the window and gaze out at the heaving street. When he spoke, a few minutes later, he had changed the subject completely. 'You know, in 1939, the Kolis in this village got two mechanized boats. They were the first ones we ever had,' he said, his voice now softer and more wistful. 'So a large group of us went down to Malvan to catch mackerel. That was the biggest haul of mackerel Mumbai had ever seen.' He stared out of the window a while longer and then repeated what he'd said earlier. 'From our house, we could see the sea, with all the boats lined up and their flags waving. It was just beautiful.'

9
On the crafting of
a fishing boat

On the coast of the misshapen lower jaw of Gujarat, in a town called Mangrol, a long, narrow road runs from the town's centre to its incredibly cluttered harbour. For most of its length, the road is flanked by rectangular plots of land marked off from each other by high compound walls. These walls hide much of the activity happening behind them, but they cannot keep to themselves the sounds of hammering and raspy sawing, or the sight of blond beams of wood rising into the air, looking like mutant orchards of very naked trees. Occasionally these strange trees will bow and curve towards each other, tending towards definite shapes that give the game away: Here is the tip of something that resembles a prow, and there is the broad back of a stern-looking object. And about a hundred times a year, the wide metal gates to these yards will swing open, and a flatbed truck will rumble out, bearing a fully finished boat on its back, and head down the road to the harbour to set it to sea.

There is a similar but even bigger boat builders' row in the neighbouring town of Veraval, the leading producer of fish in

Gujarat. This amalgamation of yards is much less shy, free of divider walls and open for gawking. On the waterfront, one yard runs without fuss into the next, and a walk down a long chain of project lots can feel like watching a vaguely obscene boat strip-show; in stages, the craft divest themselves of their wooden planking, going from completed to semi-complete to barely clothed within a few hundred yards. The lovely, sharp smell of sawdust is everywhere, and the wooden boats are so ark-like in their shape and appearance that it isn't difficult to picture pairs of giraffes and racoons and hippopotami peering over the gunwales at the commotion below.

I visited Veraval and Mangrol during the period of limbo, full of anticipation, unique to the Indian subcontinent—when news of the monsoon's descent upon Kerala has percolated to the remainder of the country, and so when, even in Gujarat, the air can feel a few degrees cooler, purely as a consequence of monsoonal hope and imagination. In both towns, when fishing halts for the rainy season as required by law as well as by common sense, the building of fishing boats is the only related trade that continues apace. 'Actually, it's even more hectic now,' one boat builder told me, 'because all the fishermen bring in their boats out of the water, to be repaired, repainted, weatherproofed, all that stuff.'

This unnatural reverse exodus of some boats, from water to land, had started. In one large area of the Mangrol dockyard, a crane had been lifting fishing boats off flatbed trucks all morning and setting them down gently on block supports, their rudder blades choked solid with plastic bags. Here they would wait under tarpaulins for the end of the monsoon, to be worked upon and restored, until they could go out to sea again. There were a dozen boats perched on blocks already. 'In a day or two, this entire space where we're standing will be filled with boats,' my boat builder predicted.

There are a lot of boats here—squads of operational fishing and cargo vessels, of course, but also many half-constructed boats, skeletons waiting to be fleshed out. As the state with the longest coastline, Gujarat, not surprisingly, is one of the country's top producers of fish, but most of its produce is promptly iced and trucked off to other parts of India. Few Gujaratis—one in ten, according to one statistic—eat any meat at all, so the state's relationship with fishing is almost a purely commercial one; Gujarat's fish now appear even in markets in Kolkata, not to mention most of the rest of North India. There is a thriving industry in the catching of fish, but also in the building of boats to catch fish, and this part of Gujarat is one of the premier commercial boat building sites in India. Since 1947, over 16,200 boats have been registered in Veraval and Mangrol combined, and nearly a quarter of that number is still active in Veraval. These are mostly wooden boats—roughly 1,200 fibreglass craft to 3,750 wooden ones in Veraval, because fibreglass is considered tackier and inferior—and so mostly manufactured in the immediate vicinity. The boat builders of Veraval and Mangrol, and of Porbandar further to the north, call themselves consummate fishing boat specialists; they tackle some cargo carrier projects, by apparently just scaling up their fishing boat designs, but the real hub of the cargo boat-building trade is the district of Kutch, elsewhere in Gujarat.

I had come to Gujarat because I had heard and read so many stories about the fishing boat builders of Veraval and Mangrol: about how carpenters had been building fishing boats here for many generations; how they continued to build them to exactly the same design; how the entire boat was worked by hand, without a power tool in sight; how the engine was the boat's only recent, grudging concession to modernity. (One source may even have murmured something about a long chain of boat design stretching right back to the Indus Valley Civilization.) Looking back, I'm not sure now what I had expected. I seem to remember visions of a little Mediterranean boat yard basking in the sun, where a carpenter with a practitioner's deep knowledge of naval history worked languidly on the construction of a boat a year. Possibly I had imagined meeting an old boat-building codger who would complain about the decline of his art and about how power tools had sullied his trade now, just because these damn youngsters wanted to build faster to make more money, and that's all they were interested in anyway, money, money, money. I know certainly that I had expected the gentle, educational pace of artisanry rather than the cold gallop of industry. And I know that I hadn't expected so many boats.

Over the last three decades, the boat-building business has been nurtured, by the government and aid agencies and private well-wishers, into thriving life. On one particular stroll through the Veraval waterfront, I counted thirty structures in advanced stages of boatishness, plus numerous other avant-garde installations of wood that would become boats in the very near future. My fellow flâneur, a gangly, bearded man named Allah Rakha Sheikh (and nicknamed, as seemed the case with one out of every three middle-aged men I met, 'Bapu'), pointed out boats that would go to Maharashtra or Karnataka, and he introduced me to the leading suthars—generic carpenters turned specialized boat builders—we encountered. The seven biggest suthars in Veraval, Bapu estimated, employ more than a thousand people between them; next to fishing itself, this is one of the town's most vital industries.

If anything, in fact, it is too vital, because there is only so much harbour to go around. Just calling the Mangrol harbour 'cluttered,' as I did earlier, cannot sufficiently describe the astoundingly close packing of craft or my difficulty in spotting even a few contiguous inches of water. Veraval's harbour, built for two thousand boats, now somehow accommodates double that. 'There is a difference between having two sons and having six sons, don't you think?' Veraval's port officer, C. M. Rathod, told me with winning wisdom, explaining that just as the more potent father would have a harder time housing his offspring, so the port authority struggled to find room for its boats. In 2003, a Gujarat Maritime Board amendment prevented fishermen with one boat from buying another. Five years later, after terrorists sailed into Indian waters from Karachi, took control of a Gujarat-registered boat called *Kuber*, and ploughed onwards to attack Mumbai, the hand dispensing new boat registrations closed even tighter. In Veraval in fact, Rathod said, the process had ceased altogether, precipitated by security concerns but fortuitously also addressing the space crunch. Naturally, this cramped the style of the region's boat builders, but not as much as one would think. An old trick came to the rescue yet again: Boat owners continued to commission boats and then simply carried forward the registration of their old vessel to the new. Same identity, but a younger, bigger, stronger body—a transposition that mouth-wateringly approaches immortality.

To build your first boat, I thought to myself in Veraval, must be to move along a chain of seeming impossibilities. There is initially the envisioning of a boat where there is nothing but air, and then the fitting of planks to snatch that boat's shape out of the air, without any frame or mould to serve as template. There is the counter-intuitive bending of planks, where a long piece of flattened, arced wood can be equally strong at every point along its curvature. There is the effort to make watertight and seamless a structure with so many, many seams. There is the slow bulking of the vessel, accompanied by the dawning bewilderment at the laws of physics that allow something so big and heavy to float on water. Maritime historian Basil Greenhill, in his definitive *Archaeology of the Boat*, compared boat building at its best to 'an act of sculpture,' but it's actually that and a little more; Rodin didn't have to float his *Thinker* out to sea and bring back a couple of tons of mackerel in it.

Murjibhai Koria built his first boat twenty-five years ago. His father had been a farmer, and Koria himself, having acquired a bachelor's degree in Gujarati, had wanted to be a schoolteacher. 'But there was more promise in this, if you get what I'm saying,' he said, gesturing at the half-built boat that stood in his yard in Mangrol. Koria was perspiring hard, and streaks of sawdust-infused sweat ran down the sides of his round face; he had just been working over a saw stationed in the sunniest spot in the yard, guiding planks through its teeth to emerge curved and ready for the belly of the boat. (It was the trickiest part of his job, he said.) We stood now in patchy shade, which is all that an incomplete boat can offer, but Koria still shielded his eyes with one hand and squinted at me as he spoke.

In Mangrol, a yard full of incomplete boats

The boat under development was a thirty-ton fishing craft, being constructed (at a price, inclusive of the engine, of Rs 25 lakhs) for a local fishing boat-owner named Veljibhai Dhanjibhai. 'He already owns four boats,' Koria said. Then he looked up at the superstructure and said: 'Can you believe that, when I first began doing this, we used to sell the boats for Rs 20,000 apiece? And that was such a lot of money at that time.' He sounded almost incredulous of the contours of a past he had lived through. 'We'd work on a boat for six or eight months, to finish it. Now it's two-and-a-half, sometimes three months, and then it's ready for the sea.' Those first few days in the harbour, Koria said with a smile, were his favourite. 'The boat is new, so it sits high on the water, and you can see nearly all the work we've put in. Then the wood begins to drink water, and it settles lower and lower.'

Half a dozen years after he has sent a boat out, it will be sent back to him, like an errant child from boarding school, to be whipped back into shape. 'The international and local woods,' he explained, pointing first to the light-coloured Malaysian sal used for the superstructure and then to the dense babul that forms the boat's inner ribs, 'somehow don't go well together. So after six or seven years, we have to tear out the insides and replace it all with fresh wood.' Another six or seven years after that, the boat will have sailed the course of its active life, and it will return one last time to Koria, reeking of fish and utterly spent, its spare parts and healthier wooden sections to be donated like organs into the therapy of Koria's next case.

During this lecture-demonstration on the life cycle of a fishing boat, an aged, pot-bellied man with a pitted face had come into the yard, hollered a merry greeting across to Koria, and then started to stride around the boat, examining it with avid interest. Dhanjibhai ('Please call me Bapu') liked to drop in every day to look at his eventual boat, he said after he had finished his rounds and walked over to us. 'That way, I feel like I know the boat well even on its first day in the water.'

Dhanjibhai came from a lineage of fishermen, and he had begun fishing very early in his youth. 'A long time ago, before engines, I used to fish in those boats made out of a single log,' he told me. In the sun, his pockmarked face offered a checkerboard texture of light and shadow. 'You could only go out to a depth of around a hundred feet in that kind of boat. I fished in those for almost twenty years.' When they went out for a night of fishing, they would cast a net into the waters and then row rough circles around it, to keep the boat from drifting away. If they ate, they ate with one hand and rowed with the other. 'In November and December, our blankets would be soaked from the spray. It would become incredibly cold.' Then he unshipped a toothy grin and said: 'All in all, when we began to get engines for our boats in the 1960s, we were pretty happy about it.'

I had heard about these dug-out boats earlier in that day, when I had met Ramji Gohil, the head of the local fishermen's association in Mangrol. Amidst a flood of propaganda about Mangrol's productivity, he had managed to inform me that the large logs for these boats used to arrive from Mangalore, in Karnataka, where the dug-out was virtually an institution. It had puzzled me when I heard it from Gohil, and it puzzled me now. 'Dug-outs?' I asked Dhanjibhai. 'But haven't you always fished in boats that looked like this one? I thought, in Gujarat, they always made fishing boats that looked like this.'

'Fishing boats?' Dhanjibhai said. 'No, no, we all definitely fished in dug-outs.' He thought for a few seconds, as if double-checking his memory to make sure, and then said: 'The only boats that looked like this were the cargo boats.'

So that was the answer, neatly reversed: It was not that the boat builders of Veraval and Mangrol were scaling up their fishing boat designs into cargo boats, but that they were scaling down their cargo boat designs into fishing boats. The structural ancestors of these fishing boats I was seeing were the cargo carriers that had, since the first millennium BCE, worked trade routes back and forth across the Arabian Sea, into the Persian Gulf, and perhaps even all the way to the Horn of Africa. The tradition of building these boats had continued in boatyards around Gujarat, preserving its techniques with such fidelity that they would often be the subject of marvelling remarks in the journals of visitors—as, for instance, in the memoirs of John Splinter Stavorinus, Esq.

In the latter half of the eighteenth century, Stavorinus, a Dutch rear-admiral, had traipsed extensively across Asia, faithfully recording his observations in three volumes of travel writing. The third of these segments of *Voyages to the East Indies* follows Stavorinus on his journey 'from Surat to Batavia, the coast of Malabar, and the Cape of Good Hope; in the years 1775–1778,' and after a chapter on Surat's Parsees and another on the city's commerce, Stavorinus comes to his own trade. 'The ships which are built here, cost, it is true, very dear, but they are able to navigate the seas for a hundred years together,' he wrote admiringly. Then, at what was called 'the English yard' in Surat, he watched a boat in the throes of its construction.

'They do not put the planks together as we do, with flat edges towards each other, but rabbet them; and they make the parts fit into each other with the greatest exactness,' Stavorinus observed. (A rabbet, I learned in Veraval, was groove cut along the longitude of a plank's edge; in cross section, a plank with a rabbet looks like a two-step staircase.) '[F]or this purpose, they smear the edges of the planks, which are set up, with red lead, and those intended to be placed next, are put upon them, and pressed down, in order to be able to discern the inequalities, which are marked by the red lead . . . they then rub both edges with a sort of glue, which becomes, by age, as hard as iron . . . after which they unite the planks so firmly and closely with pegs, that the seam is scarcely visible, and the whole seems to form one entire piece of timber.'

Stavorinus noted two other unfamiliar techniques in Surat.

The boat builders, instead of using bolts, drove iron spikes through their wood. (Even then, as with today's Malaysian sal, the timber 'must be brought hither from distant places, [making] ship-building very dear here.') Finally, into the bottom of a completed boat, its builders rubbed 'an oil which they call wood-oil, which the planks imbibe, and it serves greatly to nourish and keep them from decay,' and for pitch, 'they have the gum of a tree called *dammex*.' The boat, with a keel one hundred feet long, would cost seventy-five thousand rupees—very dear, as Stavorinus pointed out.

It is this process, in large part, which has survived in Gujarat's boat-building yards. Citing Stavorinus' account in particular, G. Victor Rajamanickam, in a book titled *Traditional Indian Ship Building*, concludes: 'Thus, we find that the boat-building techniques followed today . . . on the west coast is (sic) more or less the same form as described by our historians of the past. Not only have the ancient techniques survived . . . but many technical terms about boats are still in use, i.e. *pathan*, the term for keel, *nal* for the bow, and *vak* for the crossbeam and *percha* for the rudder.'

In Veraval, thanks to Bapu, I wheedled my way for hours at a time into the yards of two master boat builders. The first of these, Mohammad Razzaq, was a busy man, made surly by his busyness. In a yard that sat at the very edge of the water in the harbour, he commanded a large crew that seemed to need perpetual oversight; during our conversations, as we sat on one of the crosswise ribs inside his half-constructed boat, his eyes would skip constantly from me to one of the workers around him. Once, he even leaped to his feet in the middle of a sentence, hurried away to a woodworker in a corner of the boat's shell, wrenched the tool from his hands, and put him through a quick show-and-tell session on how to do the job the right way.

Razzaq is part of his family's third generation of boat

builders, and he began working on boats even as a boy. 'I did all this menial work too,' he said, pointing to the men around him chipping and smoothing away wood with adzes of varying sizes. 'It's the only way to learn the entire craft. Otherwise, you get no formal instruction in this. I just had to pick it up as I worked.' Here he paused to yell some exotic obscenities at a man with a hammer, pounding away so diligently that he had already sunk the nail into the beam and was now denting the wood around it. 'This is a medium-sized cargo boat,' Razzaq resumed, when the air had turned less blue. 'A small fishing boat, with six carpenters or so, I can build in three months. If we do a really big carrier of many hundred tons, with even twenty carpenters, it could take two years. So we do a mix of both.'

This particular boat sat propped on wooden supports— sometimes solid, pillar-like logs but just as often stacks of leftover pieces that seemed in danger of disassembling at any moment. The teak keel, laid first, was the only section of wood that had already been oiled and varnished, and it shone a rich, dark brown in contrast to the dull yellow-white of the rest of the boat. ('It's tradition,' Razzaq said. 'We always oil the keel before we begin work on the rest of the boat.') For a fishing boat, the keel consists only of one long segment of wood; for a carrier, such as this one, the keel was three such segments, bolted together end to end.

And, myth-bustingly, there were power tools. There was one hefty power saw outside the boat, to cut planks down to size. There were a couple of drills in use, whining away as they chewed into the meat of the wood. There was one electric sander. There were white power cords all over the place, like spilled spaghetti, finding their way ultimately to switch boards and electricity outlets temporarily screwed into the keel. I asked Razzaq when he had started using power tools, and he looked at me strangely and said: 'Years ago. It cuts our work time down so much. Why wouldn't we use them?'

Why indeed? Once the question is asked, it feels hypocritical for us in the cities—ever-ready beneficiaries of the efficiencies of technology—to warm to and celebrate stories of the old-fashioned (and so mostly menial) methods still in use in India's smaller towns and villages. (For many of us, this is, I am convinced, part of a broader attempt to fool ourselves into thinking that we really would opt for the 'simpler' life if only we had the choice—when, actually, we do have the choice, and we just don't want to give up our cell phones and power saws.) The truth, of course, is that the purely artisanal can no longer survive as a profession today—as a hobby or a subsidized exhibit of nostalgia, maybe, but not as a career that puts kids through school and savings in the bank. The old codger grumbles about new-fangled methods, in part, only because they're putting him out of business. In reality, Mohammad Razzaq and other suthars could either have bought these electric tools to remain full-fledged boat builders, or they could have persisted with hand-cutting their logs of wood, taken triple the time to build a boat, and watched fishermen buy fibreglass instead. This kind of dilemma is no dilemma at all; the power saw is, in that sense, now a part of the natural order of things.

But it isn't as if there is nothing of the past left to see. Stay long enough in Veraval's boat-building yards, and talk enough to the carpenters on their shifts, and look around closely enough, and you'll spot little remnants of the observations of Stavorinus and others. Razzaq's workers still hammered at iron nails the length of my palm, although they also used nuts and bolts for some purposes. They also showed me tubs of shark oil and of dammar gum ('dum-dum,' one carpenter called it), both of which they used to waterproof the bottom of their boats. The dammar gum is of the '*dammex*' tree that *Voyage to the East Indies* mentions, but even five centuries before Stavorinus, Marco Polo had learned of similar anointments to the boats plying the

Arabian Sea. Some were 'smeared with an oil made from the fat of fish,' and others coated with 'quick-lime and hemp, which latter they cut small, and with these, when pounded together, they mix oil procured from a certain tree, making of the whole a kind of unguent, which retains its viscous properties more firmly, and is a better material than pitch.'

During one of my vigils at Razzaq's yard, I watched two men mark off a section of planking, to be cut to fit a particular slot in the boat's frame. With a length of thin rope, they obtained the measure of that slot, and then they carried the rope over to the wood. One man held his end firmly down, while the other strode along the plank, chalking the measured length of the rope. When he finally reached his end of the rope, the chalk traced a long, straight line, ready to be guided into the saw. Except that, the first time, the line wasn't quite as straight as the men would have liked it, and after standing over it in hushed conference for a few seconds, they began at opposite ends and scurried towards each other, carefully brushing the chalk off with their hands as if they were flicking insects off the wood. Then they repeated the exercise until they got it right. It was a charming, inch-tape-less vignette.

A short walk from Razzaq's lot was the yard of Arjanbhai, another of Bapu's friends. Arjanbhai's yard was quieter and less manic, and Arjanbhai himself, working as he was on just a single small fishing boat at the time, was more patient and welcoming. (He also had a dark sense of humour. 'You know why a wooden boat is better than a fibreglass one?' he said. 'If it sinks, you can always hold on to the planks and save yourself. But if it's fibreglass . . .') The boat, nearly completed, sat in the dead centre of the rectangular yard; its two future owners sat in plastic chairs, under the bulk of their vessel, trees managing to provide shadow long after they had been stripped of foliage and turned into lumber.

Via a rickety ladder, Arjanbhai led me on to the boat's planked deck, smelling strongly of that morning's coat of linseed oil. He pointed out two perfectly square gaps—one leading to a hold for ice, and the second to a larger hold to store fish—that would soon be covered by metalled hatches. Another gap in the deck waited for the installation of the boat's wheel; peering through it, I could see the drilled-out hole in a longitudinal beam far below, through which the wheel would connect with the rudder. Within the boat's innards, a carpenter was laying down pre-cut sheets of plywood to serve as the floors of the holds.

'Is there anything happening today that is being done exactly as it was a century or two ago?' I asked Arjanbhai out of curiosity.

Oh definitely, Arjanbhai said, and led me back down the ladder and towards the prow of the boat. Here, a boy in his late teens was dipping strands of braided cotton into a mix of oil and resin, and then inserting the strands into the crevices between the planks with the help of a chisel and a mallet, pounding them into place until the crevices were full. He worked with his face turned up, and drops of resin-oil mixture fell occasionally onto his forehead or his cheeks, mixing with his perspiration and running down to stain the collar of his shirt an even deeper brown. And thus he caulked the boat into absolute watertightness, the cotton and resin-oil unique to the boats of the Arabian Sea, but the technique itself, in its essence, exactly the same as that used for hundreds of years by boat builders all over the world.

Choosing one particularly sweltering afternoon, Bapu decided that I should visit the Shiva temple at Somnath, less than half an hour's ride away on his motorcycle. 'I've seen it dozens of times,' he said when we reached there. 'You go on and look around. I'll wait here for you and have a Pepsi.'

It was not an afternoon conducive to temple-going. I walked barefoot towards the shrine in an overheated daze, lurching painfully from burning flagstone to burning flagstone, and standing much longer than necessary in the occasional puddle of shade. Indoors, the temple seemed too crowded for a weekday—too crowded, in any case, for my patience, which like paper had been charred into brittleness by the sun—so I ducked out of the southern entrance and walked towards the edge of the very low bluff upon which the temple sits. I could hear the ocean even some distance from the perimeter railing, and once at the edge, the wind arriving cool and fresh off the sea, I felt calmer and more comfortable.

From the railing, I could look down at the small beach of blackened sand just at the foot of the bluff, and at the dense crowd that slowly roasted itself upon that sand. Above me, to my right, stood a remarkable stone pillar with an arrow that pointed out to sea; a legend, inscribed on the pillar, states that there is no other land between that arrow on the seashore and the northern lip of Antarctica. As on that bench in Diamond Harbour, in West Bengal, I stood again on a cusp. To my right was the unimaginable vastness of the open ocean, running past Arabia and Africa to stretch nearly all the way to the South Pole, the bottom of the world. To my left was all the hulking peninsular mass of India.

I stood at the railing for twenty minutes, staring into the infinite distance, until my feet complained. Then I made my way out of the temple and towards the parking lot, where Bapu was waiting near his motorcycle.

AFTERWORD

A few weeks after I'd returned from Gujarat, somebody happened to ask me what had surprised me most about my travels. It was a wisely worded question. Travel does nothing better than swinging a wrecking-ball into even your most meagre expectations. A place is always hotter or wetter or colder or drier than you suspect it will be; people will always turn out to have stories different from the ones you set out to hear; a society will, when you think you've got it all figured out, always turn itself inside-out like a sock, to reveal its frayed threads, its seams, its patterns of stitch work. The real process of discovery works not by revealing things you knew nothing about, but by revealing how wrong you were about what you did know.

The standard India story rightly emphasizes the gamut of differences from one state to the next. What struck me more, however, were the similarities of the coastal communities I visited, right around the country. A fisherman in Tamil Nadu looked very much like a fisherman in Gujarat, as slender as a mast and scorched dry by sun and salt. Already fragile livelihoods rose and fell with the fishing calendar. The histories of these societies, the first points of contact for maritime explorers coming to India, proved uniformly cosmopolitan, readily absorbing the influences they received. And throughout my travels, I encountered the fisherman's quietly articulated complaints against the modern age. In a common paradox, traditional fishing families were moving away from their trade, and yet harbours and ports were crammed past capacity with motorized fishing boats and trawlers. The owners of these craft were pure businessmen, concerned with volumes above all else. The inevitable consequences, everywhere I went, were overfishing and degraded coastal waters, stripped as thoroughly of their riches as a king consigned to exile.

The rhythms and habits of lives on the coast are so alike because they have been shaped by the same force of nature. For all its variations in salinity or fauna or temperature gradient, the sea is the same everywhere. It is moody, dangerous and inscrutable, imposing particular disciplines upon those who depend on it. In fact, now that farmers have controlled their land—or doped it into submission, depending on your point of view—with chemistry and genetics, the fishermen are the last remaining people in India to work closely and daily in an untamed natural world. The GPS may have replaced the compass and the stars, and the engine may have helped to permanently stow oars and sail. But as Yeshi Chimbaikar pointed out to me in Mumbai, short of dredging the ocean floor, there isn't yet a substitute for spending long hours on the water, praying for a misguided fish to wander onto a line or into a net. Fishing is still elemental in the most elemental sense of the word—an activity composed of water and air and light and space, all arranged in precarious balance around a central idea of a man in a boat, waiting for a bite.

ACKNOWLEDGEMENTS

My gratitude is due first to Kamini Mahadevan at Penguin Books India, with whom I started talking about this project, who encouraged it along during its bleakest patches, and who waited courageously as I overshot deadline after deadline with consummate ease. I should also mention my employers at *Mint*, who supported my working on this book even as I held down a day job with them.

Any book involving this much travel could not have happened without the help of vast numbers of people. Many of them star as characters within these chapters. Many more were anonymous, simply flitting in and out of this journey like moths across a windshield. This is true especially of lower-level government and civic officials, who are ordinarily much maligned in India, but who were unfailingly generous in the small towns and villages that I visited.

My particular thanks:

In **West Bengal:** To the Pals, for their hospitality, and to Nilanjana, for so much more; to Atri Bhattacharya; to Chefs Sharad Dewan and Vasanthi.

In **Andhra Pradesh:** To Shalini and Guru; and to P. Anil Kumar for his photographic expertise.

In **Tamil Nadu:** To Joe D'Cruz, for all his knowledge and patience and help; to Amalraaj Fernando, for giving of his time so unstintingly.

In **Kerala:** To Freddy Koikaran, for proving to be such a great travel companion, and to Neesha, for loaning me Freddie for a week; to Ashima and Arjun and their two lovely daughters; to Mahesh Thampy and to Madhu Madhavan.

In **Karnataka:** To Vasudev Boloor and his family; to Shamanth Rao, V. V. Ramanan, and Jaideep Shenoy.

In **Maharashtra:** To Peter Baptista, Emil and Yvan Carvalho; to Danny Moses.

In **Goa:** To Maria Couto, for her invaluable insights; to Danny Moses again; to Claude Alvares; to Ravi Venkatesh and Vipin Kannoth; and especially to George Francis Borges.

In **Mumbai:** To Harini and Nithin, of course; to Vibha and Dilip D'Souza; to Naresh Fernandes and Mario Rodrigues; to Yeshi Chimbaikar and Gobind Patil.

In **Gujarat:** To Allah Rakha Sheikh, more gratitude than I can express; to Achyut Yagnik and Ashok Shrimali at SETU; to Lotika Varadarajan, for all her time and patience.